DOMINICAN REPUBLIC

BY
RYAN LEVITT

Produced by
Thomas Cook Publishing

Written by Ryan Levitt

Original photography by Ethel Davies

Original design by Laburnum Technologies Pvt Ltd

Editing and page layout by Cambridge Publishing Management Limited, Burr Elm Court, Caldecote CB3 7NU Series Editor: Penny Isaac

Published by Thomas Cook Publishing
A division of Thomas Cook Tour Operations Limited

PO Box 227, The Thomas Cook Business Park, Unit 15/16, Coningsby Road, Peterborough PE3 8SB, United Kingdom
E-mail: books@thomascook.com
www.thomascookpublishing.com
+44 (0)1733 416477

ISBN: 1-841574-51-1

Text © 2005 Thomas Cook Publishing
Maps © 2005 Thomas Cook Publishing
First edition © 2005 Thomas Cook Publishing

Head of Thomas Cook Publishing: Chris Young
Project Editor: Charlotte Christensen
Project Administrator: Michelle Warrington
DTP: Steven Collins

Printed and bound in Spain by: Grafo Industrias Gráficas, Basauri

Contents

Introduction

The Dominican Republic is now the most popular destination in the Caribbean, with more hotel rooms than any other country in the region. Twenty years ago tourism was only just beginning to emerge as a viable economic option. Today, however, the country is a tourism leader, drawing in a wide cross-section of moneyed visitors and budget-conscious holidaymakers, all looking for the perfect sunny destination.

Outdoor adventure in a Caribbean setting

Welcoming the world

The Dominican Republic offers it all – great music, friendly people, stunning beaches, delicious cuisine and amazing outdoor adventures. This is the only country in the Caribbean where you could potentially hike up a mountain, go white-water rafting and soak up the sun on an untouched stretch of sand, all within a 24-hour period.

In addition to offering up the best range of hotel accommodation in the Caribbean, the Dominican Republic has also earned a good reputation for its developments of all-inclusive resorts. Playa Dorada is probably the world's best-known collection of all-you-could-want-or-need properties; these resorts are ideally suited to the traveller who wants complete relaxation and no hassle. For the five-star patron, the choices are endless. Casa de Campo in La Romaná is so fancy that it was where pop singer Michael Jackson chose to marry Lisa Marie Presley – luckily the hotel has lasted a lot longer than their ill-fated marriage.

More than a suntan

The Dominican is a lot more than just sun, sea and sand – it's also the birthplace of Old-World exploration in the New World. It was in this country that Christopher Columbus established North America's first-ever European settlement. You can still see remnants of his influence in Parque Nacional La Isabela, located on the island's north coast, west of Puerto Plata.

Shopping

The Dominican is a shopper's paradise. A recognised leader in the global supply of amber, the island produces exquisite examples of this golden-hued, semi-precious stone, often with trapped insects featured in the deadly sap! Another item to add to your shopping list is larimar, a blue stone that is reminiscent of turquoise. Only in the Dominican Republic can this ocean-like rock be mined.

Smokers, especially fans of the old stogie, will find themselves right at home. After Cuba, the nation is considered one of the top producers of fine cigars. Play your cards right and you might even discover a cigar factory that supplies such recognised brands as Davidoff and Dunhill and that has private collections of fine tobacco products – you, however, will only have to pay a fraction of the price.

The fortress at San Felipe

A natural high
Blessed with natural resources, the Dominican boasts the Caribbean's highest peak, Pico Duarte. As such, the nation draws many fans of adventure travel. A forward-thinking policy to conserve vast tracts of land in the form of national parks was begun in the 1950s, and this has done much to keep the Dominican Republic happy and healthy. It has also meant that it tends to be much less affected by the deadly effects of the hurricanes that pound neighbouring Haiti.

The dazzling Dominican
So dance a merengue, rip into a bottle of rum and experience the magic of the Malecón, because you are about to embark on an adventure that combines the best of everything that this region has to offer. It may be considered one of the least expensive destinations in the Caribbean, but when it comes to selecting the perfect holiday, you will find that this glorious land offers some of the richest possibilities in the world. Enjoy!

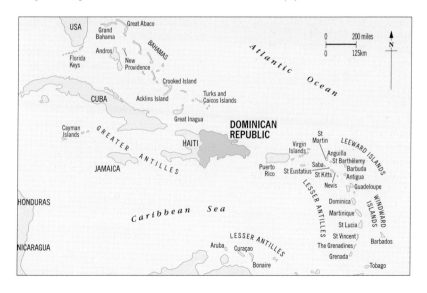

The island

The Dominican Republic is situated on the island of Hispaniola, the second largest island after Cuba in the Greater Antilles of the Caribbean. The country takes up the eastern two-thirds of the island, sharing it with the French-speaking nation of Haiti. Of Hispaniola's 76,500sq km (29,536sq miles), the Dominican Republic claims 48,500sq km (18,726sq miles), boasting almost 1,600km (1,000 miles) of beautiful coastline. To the north, the country is bordered by the Atlantic Ocean, while the Caribbean Sea sits to the south. The Mona Passage – 8,500m (27,900ft) deep – lies to the east.

Perfect palms

The population of the Dominican is just over 8.7 million people, of which 2 million live in the capital and largest city on the island, Santo Domingo. Most of the population lives along the coastline, and some in the fertile Cibao valley. The second largest city on the island, Santiago, is situated in this region, and is the country's unofficial breadbasket.

Climate

The climate of the Dominican Republic is generally warm and humid, with a constant humidity level hovering between 70 and 90 per cent at all times. This is due to its location on the edge of the tropical zone. Summer is considered the rainy season; the dry months (and consequently the peak months for tourists) fall in the winter. Traditionally, the period between May and August feature the most rainfall, while January and February are calm, clear and bright.

Precipitation affects the island in many different ways. Northeastern and southeastern trade winds significantly influence the Dominican, resulting in quite a bit of rain for the Samaná Peninsula, the eastern slopes of the Cordillera and Sierra de Baoruco and the region around San Cristóbal. Consequently, the southeast of the country (especially east of Higüey), the Enriquillo Basin and Monte Cristi are sheltered from wind and rains and boast drier than average conditions. Even in rainy season, showers – with the exception of hurricanes and tropical storms – tend to be heavy but short. Bright sunshine and calm conditions usually return after a few hours.

Winter (November to mid-April) is the peak tourist season, but the weather is generally good year-round in the Dominican. If the prospect of hurricanes frightens you, then it is best to avoid travelling between June and November. Check the Foreign & Commonwealth Office website (*www.fco.gov.uk*) for the latest updates.

Along the coast, daytime temperatures fluctuate between 27°C (80°F) and 32°C (90°F) throughout the year. At night, this figure rarely drops below 20°C (68°F). The interior is cooler, especially in the mountainous region of the Cordillera. Temperatures can fall below freezing in the higher altitudes during the winter. If you plan on trekking, it is a good idea to keep note of any forecasts, as heavy rainfall and flash flooding can cause havoc.

Swimmers will be able to enjoy a balmy water temperature of between 26°C (78°F) and 31°C (88°F) along most of the coast.

The lie of the land

The two largest cities in the Dominican Republic are Santo Domingo, which is located in the southeast of the island on the plain of Santo Domingo, and Santiago, which lies in the Cibao Valley, southwest of the main tourist centre of Puerto Plata.

Between these two major cities is the range known as the Cordillera Central (Central Mountains). The peaks reach 3,175m (10,417ft) at Pico Duarte: this is the highest point in the Caribbean. Many important rivers, including the Ozama and Chavón, can trace their source to this point.

Mountain ranges in the Dominican run northwest to southeast, extending across the coastal zone between Puerto Plata and Nagua as far as the Samaná Peninsula, a lush spit of land that extends out from the island at its northeastern tip.

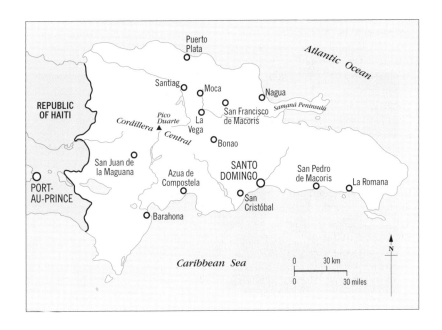

Sadly, the Dominican Republic has suffered the devastating destruction of hurricanes for many years. But unfortunately this has not led locals to prepare for the inevitable onslaughts in any constructive manner. When the high winds and pounding rain arrive (as they almost invariably do every few years or so), the effects can be fatal. Hurricane Georges killed thousands of Dominicans when it unleashed its power on the country in 1998. The entire village of Mesopotamia (pop 1,000), located in the southern foothills of the Cordillera Central, was wiped out; it was days before corpses and debris appeared more than 50km (30 miles) downstream.

What is a hurricane?

Hurricane is the name given to tropical cyclones in the Atlantic Ocean. Most hurricanes form off the coast of Africa, and start life as heavy thunderstorms. Over a timescale of anything from a few hours to a few days, these storms gradually become more intense as their wind speeds increase. As they get more powerful they move counter-clockwise across the Atlantic from east to west, continuing to build up speed and power as they are fed by warm winds and moisture.

As the storm approaches land, meteorologists will usually brand it as a tropical disturbance and issue warnings to the public. As the wind speeds increase, it becomes a tropical depression and then, when wind speeds reach between 55km/h (34mph) and 118km/h (74mph), it is known as a tropical storm. Although still below hurricane force, such storms can cause enormous devastation. Tropical Storm Jeanne proved that in 2004 when it

swept out to sea is 1km (0.625 miles) from the coast. Avoid standing near windows, as hurricane-strength winds can very easily shatter glass.

If possible, try and stock up on a week's worth of basics such as canned food and water. The Dominican is not the most disaster-conscious of nations, and in the aftermath of a hurricane the local population often face many hardships and shortages. Other things to purchase are flashlights, batteries and gasoline/oil if you have a portable generator: basics such as electricity and heating/cooling could take weeks, even months, to be re-established.

Keep informed

Make sure you are properly informed about the weather. Check the website of the Miami Herald (*www.herald.com*) (information is in the top menu) or the Foreign & Commonwealth Office (*www.fco.co.uk*) for daily updates regarding tropical storms and hurricanes that may affect the area.

decimated homes and businesses along the eastern third of the country.

When the storm reaches wind speeds of more than 120km/h (75 mph), the problems really begin. The lowest category one hurricanes can still be terrifying. Category five hurricanes, however, are rare but deadly. Hurricane Mitch, which struck in 1998, is an example of a category five storm – the final death toll from the hurricane reached more than 10,000.

What to do if you get caught

If a hurricane is predicted while you are on the island, do your best to leave. If this is not possible, head for the mountains, away from the swelling seas and pounding waves. Do not relocate to a town anywhere near a river. The minimum safe distance to avoid being

Opposite: Life goes on in the aftermath of the hurricane
Above: Ominous clouds herald the approaching storm
Right: A home ravaged by the elements

History

c. AD 200	The Ciboney Indians are driven off the island by the Tainos. The Tainos remain the dominant presence in the Dominican Republic until the arrival of Columbus almost 1,300 years later.
1492	In his search for a passage to the Orient, Christopher Columbus 'discovers' the island and renames it La Isla Española due to its resemblance in shape to Spain. Settlements are established on the north coast, which are promptly destroyed by disease and Indian attacks.
1493	Columbus founds the first permanent town in North America on the north shore of the island, east of his original settlement. He names it La Isabela in tribute to the Spanish queen.
1496	The town of La Nueva Isabela is built on the banks of the Río Ozama. Santo Domingo is founded on the west bank.
1509	Santo Domingo flourishes under the direction of Columbus's eldest son, Diego Colón.
1586	Sir Frances Drake pillages and almost destroys Santo Domingo.
1605–6	Spanish settlers are moved to the south shore from the north and west of the island in an attempt to combat smuggling. The French move in to the now-empty north region.
1620s	Large numbers of Dominicans travel to Mexico and Peru after veins of gold and silver are discovered.
1697	Spain cedes the western third of the island to France; it booms due to the sugar trade.

Taino art

La Isabela: Columbus's settlement

1795 Slave uprisings against the French elite begin to trouble the country. The French face a massive loss in income as rebels target the island's highly profitable sugar trade.

1801–4 The French Revolution prompts followers of Toussaint L'Ouverture and Jean J Dessalines to plunder and pillage the island.

1804 Dessalines proclaims independence from France and creates the first black republic in America. The new country is called Haiti.

1809 The eastern two-thirds of Hispaniola return to Spain.

1821–2 The Spanish colony proclaims independence and dubs itself the Dominican Republic. Haitian forces attack shortly afterwards.

1838 The Haitian occupation prompts writer Juan Pablo Duarte, lawyer Francisco del Rosario and soldier Ramón Mella to form the secret society known as La Trinitaria.

1844 Followers of La Trinitaria occupy the fortress of Santo Domingo and declare independence. The Dominican Republic is formed once again.

1861 President General Santana exiles the Trinitaria freedom-fighters and places the country under Spanish protection, much to the dismay of the local populace.

1863–5 Civil war breaks out. The Spanish withdraw for the final time. Independence is re-established.

1882 Ulises Heureux becomes president during a golden period in Dominican history. Booming sugar prices bring wealth to the island, albeit just to the Dominican elite. Heureux borrows millions of dollars from the United States to keep the good times rolling.

1899   Heureux is assassinated. The country enters a period of great debt that – to this day – it has yet to emerge from.

1916–24   The US government intercedes in the affairs of the Dominican Republic. New roads, communication lines and schools are built. The United States also gets its hands on large amounts of raw materials and resources. The international border between Haiti and the Dominican is reinforced after years of lax controls.

1930–61   The era of dictator Rafael Trujillo. Corruption flourishes under his control, opponents are tortured and numerous companies are transferred into the hands of family members, personally benefiting Trujillo. Propaganda programmes instituted by Trujillo shape a proud Dominican identity.

1937   Trujillo orders the slaughter of an estimated 10,000 Haitian immigrants living in the Dominican. Tensions between the two nations reach crisis levels.

1939–43   German and Austrian Jews fleeing Nazi persecution are welcomed to the island. In total, 350 families make their new home in the Dominican Republic.

1961   Trujillo is assassinated. As new leader, Joaquin Balaguer begins the long process of trying to erase Trujillo's (and his family's) influence from the country.

1962   The first democratic elections ever held in the Dominican sees Juan Bosch, the leader of the Partido Revolucinario Dominicano (PRD) become president. Seven months after taking office, a military coup drives him into exile.

An early settler

1965	Supporters of Juan Bosch take control of the capital with the assistance of a group of young colonels. Known as the 'Constitutionalists', they attempt to reinstate Bosch. Fearing a Cuba-like situation, US president Lyndon Johnson intervenes and sends in the US military to help control the situation.
1966	Joaquin Balaguer returns to the presidential office after winning the election. A pro-American, he brings numerous reforms to the country, including wage freezes and an increase in exports and foreign investment. His regime causes corruption levels to rise again, however.
1978	Antonio Guzmán, head of the social-democratic PRD party, is elected president. In 1982, Guzmán discovers that members of his family have been involved in corruption. He commits suicide. The party stays in power until 1986.
1986, 1990, 1994	After eight years of social-democratic government under the PRD party,
	Balaguer – aging but as charismatic as ever – is re-elected three more times, though the last election is subject to charges of vote-rigging.
1991	All Haitian immigrants under the age of 16 and over 60 are ordered out of the country and deported. Demonstrations and strikes ensue.
1996	The PLD party sweeps into power under the direction of new president, Leonel Fernández Reyna.
1998	Hurricane Georges destroys large parts of the country. In the Sabana Perdida shantytown alone, more than 200 people are killed. Thousands of people are left homeless.
2000	With a platform of ending corruption and helping the poor, Hipólito Mejía of the PRD becomes president.
2004	Tropical Storm Jeanne lashes the Dominican with high winds and rain. Damage to the eastern half of the island is widespread.

Governance

The Dominican Republic was founded on 27 February 1844 following years of rebellion against the influence of the Spanish and French governments. This is the day celebrated by Dominicans as their 'Independence Day', and remains a national holiday.

The legacy of Columbus lives on

Today, the country is divided into 29 provinces, plus the municipal district of Santo Domingo. Presidents are elected on a four-year term as dictated by the Republic's 1966 constitution.

The right-wing dictator Rafael Trujillo took the office of president from 1930 until his assassination in 1961. His puppet Joaquín Balaguer took over from that time until 1978. But his reign didn't end then – he was re-elected (despite widespread allegations of corruption), three consecutive times from 1986 to 1996, when he was finally defeated by Dr Leonel Fernández Reyna. At the age of 92, in the 2000 elections, Balaguer ran yet again, losing to the leader of the Partido Revolucionario Dominicano (PRD), Hipólito Mejía.

Since the country's original constitution was created in 1844, it has been amended 29 times – usually to the benefit of the party in power. The president is given many powers. In addition to being the head of state, he (or she) also functions as the commander-in-chief of the armed forces and the chief of police. Outsiders sometimes view the position as a near dictatorship.

Legislative power is assumed by the bicameral Congress, which is comprised of a Senate and a Chamber of Deputies. The Senate has 30 members while the Chamber has 130. Since 1994, voters have four votes – one each for the president, Senate, Chamber of Deputies and local district council. To win an election, the president requires an absolute majority of 50 per cent plus one, and is not permitted to serve two terms in succession.

Politics: a history

Under the Trujillo dictatorship of 1930–61, political parties were banned. Those who challenged Trujillo's leadership were often tortured, murdered or exiled in order to force their silence. Following his death, a number of parties formed rapidly in order to capitalise on the country's new-found sense of freedom. Unluckily for

The Palacio Nacional, seat of the government

Dominican citizens, most of the parties served only to benefit the party leadership, and not the bulk of the (mostly poor) population.

Today, there are three major political parties vying for the attention of the Dominican people: the right-wing Partido Reformista Social-Cristiano (PRSC), which held power for much of the last half of the 20th century under the leadership of Balaguer; the Partido Revolucionario Dominicano (PRD), a left-wing organisation founded in exile by Juan Bosch in 1939; and the Partido de la Liberación Dominicana (PLD),

created in 1974 by Bosch after he parted ways with the PRD. The PRD was voted into office in 1962. It held power for six months before American intervention exiled the party leadership. The PRD returned to power from 1978 to 1986, but faced numerous charges of corruption and suffered falling popularity. The year 2000 marked their return to the presidential office under the leadership of Mejía.

The PLD has only held the office of the president once, in 1996. Its support comes from the working classes, the poor and the intellectual community.

The Altar de la Patria (Altar of the Nation) is the last resting place of the nation's great and good

Unfortunately, its policy to cut ties with the US and attempt to distribute wealth and income fairly among all sectors of society is not supported by the international community, and in practice had devastating economic consequences during its four years in power.

Other influences in Dominican politics include the army, police, the financial elite and the Catholic Church. While the constitution does not permit interference from outside organisations or from individuals in governing the nation, the reality is often far from clear-cut. All of the above 'groups' have been involved in governing the nation at certain points in its history and they continue to have influence in contentious areas.

Economy

The main sources of revenue and income for the Dominican Republic are agriculture, tourism, and industry developed in the free trade zones. By far the most important trading partner for the Dominican is the United States.

Free trade zones were introduced by the government in order to improve the economy and entice foreign investment into local industry. Industries located in the free trade zones – and in particular textile firms – account for 79 per cent of all exports. Free trade zones (or *zonas francas*, as they are known locally) are a relatively recent addition to the Dominican economy and were brought in to replace the ailing sugar industry in the early 1980s. Sugar was once the chief source of income for the country, but was affected badly by the tumble in

prices following the introduction of corn syrup and low-calorie sugar substitutes in the late 1970s.

VOTE-RIGGING

Since the assassination of Trujillo and the return of parliamentary democracy in 1966, there have been numerous charges of conspiracy, corruption and vote-rigging. Joaquin Balaguer – the puppet president declared by Trujillo during his final few years – was the leader most often accused of election frauds. Each one of his six successful campaigns between 1966 and 1994 was marred by numerous protests and calls for vote recounts.

His final victory in 1994 was the most controversial of them all, and resulted in his resignation in 1996 following two years of investigation. The election of Hipólito Mejía in 2000 is widely considered to be the first occasion in the Dominican Republic when a president was voted in both fairly and ethically.

Since 1996, the economy has steadily improved. Unfortunately, the high debt levels faced by the government have done much to restrict economic growth. Coffee, cocoa, tropical fruit and tobacco are slowly overtaking sugar in importance, thanks to large subsidies granted by the agriculture ministry to promote their development and diversify farming.

Approximately 40 per cent of the Dominican Republic is reserved for agricultural use, of which roughly half is controlled and owned by a powerful league of a dozen elite landowners and the state. Land belonging to the state is largely composed of tracts formerly 'owned' by the dictator Trujillo and confiscated following his death.

Mineral resources and mining also bring much income into the country, thanks to large deposits of gypsum, bauxite, iron ore, platinum, rock salt and ferro-nickel. Semi-precious stones are also present in abundance, specifically in the form of larimar and amber. Mining procedures tend to be basic, and little is done by mining companies to ensure environmental co-operation.

Tourism has grown drastically in the last two decades, and is now one of the Dominican's prime sources of revenue. Between 1987 and 1993, the number of hotels in the country more than doubled. Annual tourist arrivals are now more than 2 million, thanks to the development of a plethora of all-inclusive properties. However, unfortunately for the Dominican population, most hotels are foreign-owned. Local employment is limited to entry-level, poorly paid positions, and most of the income brought in by the industry is immediately taken out of the country.

Dominicans: present and future

Less than 50 years after discovering the island, Hispaniola was faced with a major test in the form of pirate attacks. The 1540s saw hundreds of raids on the blossoming settlements that lined the coast, mostly carried out by Dutch and English privateers. The pirates had been commissioned by their governments to strike fear into the hearts of the local populace, and to wrest as much wealth away from the Spanish crown's coffers as possible. Back in the Old World, Spain was at war with the Dutch and English; the easiest way in which the northern countries could attack the military superiority of Spain was through its purse.

Fighting back

In 1541, Spain built fortifications at Santo Domingo in the form of a massive wall designed to keep rivals out. Sea travel was legally restricted to large, well-armed 'caravans' – according to Spanish law, the only way that a ship could travel across the Atlantic was if it went with a minimum of five other ships. Another move to the detriment of Santo Domingo was that of the sugar industry's 'capital' to Havana. Cuba became the major stopping-off point between Mexico, Peru and Spain, much to the dismay of Dominican traders. In order to do business with Dominican plantations, traders were forced to break off from the well-armed caravans and go it alone through pirate-choked waters. The results were often catastrophic.

Smugglers' paradise

This change in Spanish trading laws forced Dominicans to work with the pirates in order to smuggle in basic necessities. They would also sell most of their wares at seriously reduced costs to the privateers, who would sell them on in England and the Netherlands. Getting something seemed to be better than getting nothing to the Dominicans, and they did not much care which superpower benefited. By the 1550s, smuggling and contraband were the only things keeping plantation owners and the traders who worked on the north coast alive.

However, these activities were regarded by some as traitorous, and eventually northern traders were forced to relocate to the interior and south coast in an effort to prevent them smuggling. The Catholic Church played

a large part in this decision; it was concerned by the spread of Protestantism through much of the region, which had arrived thanks to the pirates who were making inroads into the country. The crown burnt most of the settlements along the north coast to the ground in an operation known as '*las devastaciones*'. The effects of this policy were felt for generations. Of the estimated 110,000 heads of cattle grazing in the region at this time, only 10,000 survived the move to the plains around Santo Domingo. By 1610, half the transplanted settlers had died of disease or starvation. Spain was never a trusted leader again, and the seeds of rebellion were sown.

French encroachment

The abandonment of the north coast also did much to foster the anti-Haitian feeling that continues to exist in the modern-day Dominican Republic. As the Spanish abandoned their formerly prosperous settlements, the French moved in – to the massive resentment of the Dominican people. French-speakers are still widely looked down upon, and tensions between Haiti and the Dominican can be largely traced back to this period in time.

Societal breakdown

The influx of large numbers of settlers combined with Santo Domingo's loss in economic importance pushed the city into a drastic decline, from which it took almost two centuries to emerge. Both black slaves and their white masters lived in abysmal conditions; this translated into a breakdown in perceived societal standards and racial hierarchy, which continues to influence race relations and attitudes today.

Opposite: Ahoy there – a modern-day pirate ship roams the high seas
Top: A pirate's lair
Below: Coins from a pirate past

Culture and festivals

The citizens of the Dominican Republic are a relaxed bunch. However, this does not mean that the people are lazy. Parties, festivals and religious occasions may halt normal business in city streets on certain occasions throughout the year, but there is still a strong sense of machismo pride that drives Dominican men to provide for their family.

The Dominican missionary Bartolomeu de las Casas

A typical tourist will not see much of the 'real Dominican' – a nation where the bulk of the population works in agricultural industries and labours from dawn to dusk to ensure a strong crop. Look beyond the veneer of street-side art-naïf sellers and rum shops, and you'll find a population that works hard, plays hard – and all to the beat of their beloved merengue music.

Nevertheless, you won't need to give a Dominican too many excuses to knock off early for the day. While the promise of a pay-cheque does much to motivate, the promise of crystal-blue waters and sun-drenched beaches does much more.

Religion

Dominicans would like to think that religion continues to play an important part in everyday life, and in many ways it does – especially when it comes to political policy-making. Over 90 per cent of the population claims to be Roman Catholic, but only a small percentage of that figure actually attends Mass on a regular basis. The low level of Church attendance has not translated into a liberalisation of the laws relating to the usual 'hot topics' of abortion and

gay rights, however. Instead, the population has tended to adopt right-wing attitudes on these subjects.

Religious education is compulsory in the Dominican school system. This dates from when Trujillo formed links with the Vatican in an effort to give his dictatorship an element of respectability.

Today, the Church is largely split down the middle into a 'high' branch and a 'low' one. The high Church is the Church of the elite, composed of archbishops and senior figures supported by the government. This is the 'strict' church of the conservatives and the moneyed classes.

Alongside this is a grass-roots 'low' Church, developed during the radical 1970s and 1980s. This Church works in the neediest communities, attempting to improve the lot of the poorest of the poor.

Voodoo and the supernatural, while superficially shunned by Dominicans, also play a major role in day-to-day life – especially amongst the minority Haitian and rural populations. Ask any Dominican if they have ever turned to a witch doctor for assistance with problems and they will probably say no… But the truth is likely to be different.

It's party time! Carnival is part of the Dominican culture

Night- and social life

If you're planning a night out on the town, you might want to catch some sleep during the day. Nightlife does not tend to get going until the wee small hours. Nightclubs and cafés may open early in the day, but you'll find them largely empty until at least 11.00pm.

This late-night mentality owes much to the weather. Siestas during the afternoon are common. The high level of humidity and balmy temperatures are absolutely energy sapping, causing many Dominicans to factor a two-hour nap into their day.

In tourist towns, early diners are a common sight, as those from northern climes plan their day around a 6.00pm mealtime. Dominicans, however, would never think about dining until at least 8.00–9.00pm. You won't have much trouble finding a place to dine earlier in the tourist hotspots, but in rural backwaters, you'd better count on having to adjust your stomach's clock.

One of the nicest things to do in any Dominican town is to take a stroll along the seaside or Malecón of a beachside community, or to the central park of a town or city in the interior. These places are always the social centres in the Dominican, and where you will find the bulk of the action. Couples courting, old men chatting, ladies gossiping and friends playing chess are common sights. Play it right and you might even be invited to join in the fun.

Major festivals

Carnival is celebrated twice (yes, twice!) a year in Santo Domingo. The first carnival occurs during the traditional Mardi Gras period, during the climax of the pre-Lent holiday. This is typically timed to coincide with Independence Day celebrations on 27 February. At this time, Carnival is also celebrated throughout the nation.

The second carnival is restricted to Santo Domingo and celebrates the republic's

Check mate: a social event

A grave ending for the early settlers

every Spanish-speaking nation are invited to perform in the Olympic Stadium in Santo Domingo. Enrique Iglesias is a recent attendee.

At the same time, Puerto Plata hosts its own cultural festival. The third week of June is reserved for live music, traditional and folk dances and song. The Fuerte San Felipe hosts most of the festivities, while a fair close to the Parque Central opens up to lovers of arts and crafts.

declaration of war against Spain on 16 August. The first carnival is always the bigger of the two, but both feature vibrant costumes, dancing, floats and wild performances.

Outside of the capital, the town of La Vega hosts a brilliant Mardi Gras-type carnival featuring famous papier-mâché masks produced by its citizens.

Merengue festivals are almost as raucous as Carnival. The most notable festival celebrating this oh-so-Dominican music form is held for two weeks at the end of July and beginning of August, along the Malecón in Santo Domingo.

Puerto Plata also hosts a festival during the first week of October. The Puerto Plata festival is slightly more interesting than the one held in the capital, due to its inclusion of local craftsmen and artisans in the festivities. This is an excellent time to pick up local souvenirs; you will be able to witness the creation of goods and speak to the artists who made them.

Three days in June are reserved for one of the world's leading celebrations of Latin music. Artists from almost

Lovable little ones

Children are loved by one and all in the Dominican, especially Dominican kids. There may be some slight resentment amongst the general population if your child decides to kick up a big fuss in public: they might be labelled a junior example of a pampered Westerner. Chivalry, however, is alive and well, so if you are pregnant or travelling with the kids, you will automatically be given a seat or priority access wherever you go.

Baseball bonanza

While not strictly qualifying as a holiday, you will find that any city with a major league baseball team will screech to a halt whenever their beloved players hit the field. You would be well advised to avoid the city neighbourhood that holds the baseball stadium when this happens, or you may be caught up in a mess of traffic and colourful chaos. If you do find yourself trapped, you have a choice: either get away from the action or grab a banner and join in the fun – but make sure you adopt the local team colours!

That Voodoo That You Do

While there are few religions that can claim to offer an alternative to Catholicism in the Dominican Republic, one such belief system is the often ridiculed, always beleaguered voodoo or *vodú* faith. Voodoo is an African-inspired religion that draws elements from a number of faiths, including Catholicism. The Dominican government condemns practitioners as barbaric, and blames Haitian immigrants on its practice within the country's borders. But voodoo as a religion predates the days when the nations of Haiti and the Dominican Republic even existed.

What is voodoo?

The mixing of African and European religions harks back to the arrival of the first African slaves, who came to the French and Spanish colonies of the Caribbean in the early 16th century. There are still large numbers of followers – even people who will claim that they are Catholics when asked – who regularly mix Taino rituals, Catholic saints and African gods in their day-to-day life.

Voodoo believers worship archetypal gods, otherwise known as *lúas*. When the Catholic Church saw that the African slaves worshipped these gods, they tried to find links between the African gods and the Catholic faith in order to facilitate conversion. In most cases, they succeeded in 'transplanting' Christian saints in favour of the existing African deities. But, in some cases the result was a mix of the two – and from this arose voodoo.

Some of the most obvious religious similarities include the Barón del Cementario (the equivalent of the Christian San Elías), who guards the graveyards, and Anaísa, the goddess of love (who is based on the Christian Santa Ana).

Persecution

Under the rule of Trujillo, practitioners had to keep their beliefs largely to themselves. Trujillo and his clan of secret police would often embark on operations to rid the Dominican of 'black' and/or Haitian influences – and this would include anything voodoo-related. In the late 1930s, voodoo followers were rounded up along the Haitian border. The Dominican population was told that they had been sent back to Haiti, when in reality they were sent to camps, tortured, or murdered, with bodies dumped in the Atlantic.

Ceremonies

Voodoo ceremonies are colourful affairs and involve speaking in tongues, trances, dancing, music and spirit possession. If you are looking to witness a ceremony, the best way to go about it is to book yourself on a tour. However, the actual 'show' is likely to be highly geared towards Western tourists and so largely inauthentic. For something a little

more genuine, make enquiries in the Haitian border towns, the mountain town of San Juan de la Maguana or the mostly black, inner city barrios of Villa Mella about whether you can see a real ceremony.

Brujos

Brujos – or witch doctors, as they are more commonly known – are linked to voodoo and are often turned to in times of crisis or difficulty. Witch doctors are believed to have amazing supernatural powers, both good and evil, and can 'cure' a wide variety of problems. Some of the most common problems with which brujos are forced to deal include the 'evil eye' and financial issues. They might also distribute love potions or cures for broken hearts.

For evidence of the country's fascination with the supernatural, take a walk to any of the mercados scattered throughout the Dominican. Inside the markets are numerous stalls and botánicas selling religious icons, tarot-like cards, herbal potions and candles. While you may look at these items as curiosities or souvenirs, please note that they are considered religious artefacts by the Dominican people.

Above: Ceremonies can combine elements of a number of different belief systems.

Impressions

The Dominican Republic is easy to get around – apart
from a couple of exceptions – thanks to a network of roads
and trails constructed by the occupying American forces at
the turn of the twentieth century. While potholes are
evident and roads quickly turn to mud in rural regions
during inclement weather, you shouldn't have too many
problems getting from A to B. The exceptions to this rule
are the border region near Haiti, and the Samaná Peninsula
jutting from the northeast corner of the country. In both
cases, the attractions are primarily rural and therefore
benefit from their inaccessibility.

Fuelling the nation's
transport

Country layout

Cities in the Dominican Republic tend
to sprawl, thanks to the numerous
barrios and poorer communities that
cling around the fringes of the suburbs.
As in most developing nations, rural
residents are being drawn to major
metropolises, due to a perceived notion
that life is 'better' there.

The three largest cities in order of size
are Santo Domingo, Santiago and
Puerto Plata. Santo Domingo is the
crown-jewel of the south coast and the
capital of the country. As one of the
oldest cities in North America, it boasts
an incredible old town and collection of
museums. Santiago is the farming centre
of the Dominican, and is one of the only
major cities located inland. The city is
spectacularly set in a valley between the
Cordillera Central and the Cordillera
Septentrional. This is the place to come
for incredible handicrafts, tobacco
products and produce. Puerto Plata, on
the north coast, is primarily associated

with tourism because of its proximity to
the vast Playa Dorada complex of all-
inclusive resorts.

On the road again

A vast system of highways or 'Carreteras'
links most of the major cities of the
country. There are five major highways
in the Dominican, of which four hug the
coastline. Carretera 1 is the major
north–south artery that links the north
coast and Santiago with the capital,
Santo Domingo, in the southeast.
Carretera 2 runs from Santo Domingo
to the Haitian border through the
Sierra de Neiba. This is the road
you will take if you are planning a
trip to Haiti, Barahona or Lago
Enriquillo.

Carretera 3 goes east from Santo
Domingo to the resort towns of La
Romana and Boca Chica. Carretera 4 is
a ring road that circles the eastern tip of
the Dominican, linking La Romana and
San Pedro de Macoris with the small,

rural communities in the Cordillera Oriental. And Carretera 5 is the major highway of the north coast, bringing together Puerto Plata with Sosúa, Cabarete and the Samaná Peninsula.

A system of roads runs between all these locations. They are of varying quality. Your map may mark a road as a major route, but don't be shocked if you find that in truth it is little more than a dirt trail with tyre grooves. A four-wheel drive is therefore a must if you want to travel around the country.

When to go

Peak season in the Dominican Republic is the winter (Nov–Apr). Tourist crowds pack the resorts and beaches during this period; the weather is usually dry and temperatures pleasant. Savvy locals flee to the less well-known communities of Barahona and Samaná during this time in order to avoid having to encounter too many foreigners. Spring and autumn are invariably pleasant. Temperatures rarely drop much below 20°C (70°F) at night, and occasional

Flamingos at the Santo Domingo zoo

Transport can often be in great demand

rainstorms leave the country feeling cool and refreshed. Be careful not to arrive too early in the autumn if you want to avoid hurricane season. Storms have been known to hit the island hard as late as October.

Crowds during this period tend to be thin on the ground, and deals can be had if you know where to look. Between May and October holiday packages can be picked up by British tourists for as little as £350 for flights and three-star, all-inclusive accommodation.

From May to September, the temperature soars and the rainy season gets into full swing. This fact should not dissuade you from booking a trip, as showers tend to end rapidly. Unfortunately, this is also hurricane season, so you do run the risk of getting trapped. Summer brings the crowds back to the island, especially during August, when many North Americans and Europeans decide to take their holidays.

To get away from the stifling heat, do as the locals do and head up-mountain to the tranquil surroundings of Constanza and the Cordillera Central. This is the best season for trekking Pico Duarte. The temperature is much more bearable in the hills during this period.

Driving in the Dominican

Driving in the Dominican Republic is legendarily awful. Road accidents cause more deaths than anything else in this country, thanks to the chaotic nature of the driving. Chock-a-block urban streets and crumbling countryside highways combine to create a highly dangerous blend.

Driving is done on the right-hand side – at least in theory. The general rule of the road is 'survival of the biggest'. If you find yourself being trailed by a large truck or transporter, then pull over to let them pass if you want to see your next birthday. As for driving at night, don't do it. Only the clinically insane would ever contemplate doing so, and that includes the locals.

Getting around

Getting around the Dominican is surprisingly cheap and efficient, as long as you aren't planning on renting a car. Car rental agencies charge premium rates in the Dominican, and you are well advised to avoid renting, unless either you have money that you are happy to spare, or you are planning a trip into the rural interior.

For short distances, taxis – but only of the official, licensed kind – are your best bet. If you are approached by a tout for your business at a major tourist point, the sensible course is to politely say no and find the nearest rank. Prices may be higher, but your journey will be much safer and more comfortable.

For longer trips, buses are highly recommended. Schedules run very close to what is posted, and the actual vehicles are comfortable and air-conditioned. When booking your trip, try and book with one of the two major operators, Metro Bus or Caribe Tours. Almost all major locations are linked with each other, so you should have no problem putting an itinerary together, no matter how obscure your final destination may be.

Pollution and litter

If you're used to clean streets and tree-lined avenues, then you may be in for a shock. The streets of the Dominican's major cities sometimes resemble a refuse dump, and the paralysing traffic does little to help the situation, with air pollution rising to levels that asthmatics may find difficult to deal with – especially in the older and more closed-in sectors of Santo Domingo. When everything becomes a bit overwhelming, it is best just to flee to the more subdued and less crowded countryside.

Sadly mountain trails are also slowly becoming polluted, thanks to thoughtless trekkers who do nothing to ensure the removal of their waste. Please try and think of the people who will be following in your footsteps, and of the environment, and keep your rubbish with you until you find a bin.

Water supplies and refuse disposal is extremely limited in the major resorts. Try and limit your rubbish and use of water as much as possible to save precious resources.

Architecture

The history of the Dominican Republic stretches as far back as 1492, when the island of Hispaniola was discovered by Christopher Columbus during his search for a passage to the Orient. Remnants of Columbus's original settlement at La Isabela are still evident, providing a lasting reminder of the Old World's early influence on New World architecture.

Museo Alcázar de Colón

Early aesthetics

The finest period in the Dominican's architectural past was during the first 50 years of the 16th century. During this time the conquering Spaniards sought to create designs that reflected their perceived glory in the New World. Buildings were experimental (for their time) and reflected Spanish sensibilities and tastes.

In 1502, Santo Domingo was founded. It was laid out in a grid formation in accordance with the urban-planning theories that were popular at the time. The city hall and cathedral were placed in the middle of the settlement, directly on the main square or park, and the blocks surrounding this were reserved for religious orders. Areas beyond this were reserved for the conquistadors and elites, in a strict hierarchy based on rank and class.

The grid pattern allowed for the continual growth and expansion of the city far into the future, and served as the basis on which all Latin American cities were developed from that time. This grid-pattern theory was eventually codified into Spanish law in 1573.

Building a capital

Once one of North America's richest cities, Santo Domingo is packed with architectural treasures that act as a testament to the vast wealth that has passed through the metropolis. The old town is a UNESCO World Heritage Site, and boasts brilliant examples of everything from early 17th-century colonial to Cuban Victorian styles.

In the early years of its formation, Spanish sculptors flocked to the city to help build the numerous stone-vaulted cathedrals, churches, monasteries and hospitals that various religious orders demanded. Secular buildings and fortifications also required their attention, and this resulted in decades of employment for these much-in-demand craftsmen. Almost all buildings were constructed using brick, stone, or a combination of the two. In many cases, indigenous products were completely ignored in favour of expensively imported construction materials from Spain.

As in Spain, the architecture of the age drew much from Gothic Isabelline fashions. As shifts in taste occurred in the mother country, so did a shift in tastes in the Dominican. In all cases, however, slight variations from the norm in Dominican buildings gave regional architecture a certain sense of freedom lacking in European design. One of the best examples of this creative expression occurred in the 1620s, when Diego Colón's residence, the Casa de Almirante, was built. In traditional Spanish palaces of the time, doors opened around a private internal courtyard to ensure seclusion and security. Colón, however, chose to open his home up by installing a double loggia on both sides of his residence, which opened out to provide him with views of the city and the river.

Religious structures tended to stick more to traditional designs. The main cathedral featured a rectangular ground plan with a polygonal apse and broad central nave exactly twice the length of the aisles and lateral chapels. This design plan served as a template for almost all the churches in Latin America built during the period.

The decline and fall

As Santo Domingo lost economic importance in the mid-16th century, so it also lost its way architecturally. A number of events conspired to damage the city: these included hurricanes, earthquakes and Francis Drake's attack of 1586. Limited resources meant that the damage could not be fixed, and as a result the city was left to rot for the next 300 years.

The bulk of exciting architecture occurred outside of the cities, in the form of beautiful plantations built by the wealthy classes, most of which have

A shaded corner in the old town

now disappeared due to shoddy construction or because of limited resources. The buildings tended to be designed more for show than for longevity.

The arrival of independence in 1844 did little to improve the situation, as the nation focused its attention on reinforcing fortifications and building functional – and rather boring – private housing. The biggest alterations to Santo Domingo came in the form of the widened avenues and pleasure parks designed to reflect a French aesthetic.

Trujillo's folly

As with most dictators, Trujillo was a firm believer in constructing monumental buildings to reflect his grandeur. The project for which he is probably best known is the massive Columbus memorial lighthouse, known as the Faro a Colón. The construction of this white elephant took more than 60 years. It began in 1927 after the

San Felipe Fort overlooks the bay at Puerto Plata

Dominican Republic, with the backing of the American government, raised a loan to finance a major architectural competition to find a design. Trujillo saw the lighthouse as a chance for his nation to reclaim trade dominance in the Caribbean. For Trujillo, a lighthouse represented a beacon for ships and planes; it would also act as a monument to the Dominican Republic's historic and symbolic significance as the

The Glorieta Pavilion on the Amber Coast

The colourful houses of Santo Domingo

location of Christopher Columbus's first settlement in the New World.

More than 450 architects from 48 countries submitted their plans for the lighthouse for the first round of judging in 1929. The winner was selected from a shortlist of ten finalists by a panel of well-known judges, including Frank Lloyd Wright, at a meeting in Rio de Janeiro in 1931. The winner's name was John Gleave. He was a young British architect with few notable projects on his limited CV.

In describing the lighthouse to the judging panel, Gleave told them that it was an Egyptian sphinx, modern abstract, a geologic formation and an Aztec serpent all combined into one structure, thus making it all things to all people. It was not, however, a working lighthouse. Gleave envisioned beams of light illuminating the night sky, acting as a guide for night-flying aircraft – but it was more than this. The beams were

also intended as a metaphor for the way Columbus brought Christianity to illuminate the Americas – a fact that blended perfectly with Trujillo's racist and elitist policies. Not for him any discussion about the effects of colonialism!

After years of fund-raising, construction finally began in 1949, but the next 30 years saw numerous delays, and the establishment of shantytowns around the building site. Construction did not move forward at any real pace until the 1980s, when the Dominican government, under the leadership of Balaguer, demanded that the lighthouse be completed in time to tie in with the quincentennial of Columbus's landfall. The monument was finally inaugurated in 1992. By this time, however, lighthouses were a thing of the past and the symbolic meaning behind the structure was lost to all but a few.

Modern madness

Trujillo's preoccupation with the
lighthouse, combined with devastating
poverty, translated into a complete lack
of development or interest in a national
architectural movement. Following
Trujillo's assassination in 1961, this
pattern did not alter much, as there
was little desire to develop a Dominican
aesthetic – most new buildings
borrowed from outside influences
and trends in an effort to become
more international in focus. The
capital city saw the construction
of a number of concrete and glass
buildings taken directly from the Le
Corbusier school of design, usually with
an exotic twist to make it 'Dominican'.
One such example of this concept is the
cathedral of Nuestra Señora de la
Altagracia in Higüey.

The 1980s saw the first wave of
Dominican architects to have a say in
the design of their country. In most
cases, historical and regional styles
have been shunned in favour of a
postmodernist formalism. This is
primarily due to a lack of state

investment in grand projects, and the
emergence of a wealthy class influenced
heavily by internationalism. Most
commissions exist in the form of
resorts, private homes, clubs and tourist
hotels that favour a combination of
colonial-inspired looks with locally
designed goods. The Santo Domingo
Country Club, with its colonnades,
latticework and wooden balconies,
is a prime example of this mishmash
of styles.

Corporate buildings, however,
continue to be built with international
ideals in mind – that is, the classic
combination of steel, concrete and
mirror glass in a rectangular structure.

Outside Santo Domingo

Outside the capital, aesthetics depend
on when each region had the greatest
economic success. Santiago and Puerto
Plata benefited from blossoming trade
in the late 19th century and their
notable buildings reflect this financial
boom. As sugar prices rose, so did
buildings within their borders. Look
behind the decay in both cities and
you'll spot Cuban Victorian buildings in
addition to Caribbean gingerbread, as
well as pure Victorian (especially
centred around Puerto Plata's Parque
Central) and Art Deco.

To the dismay of many islanders, San
Pedro de Macoris was the first city to
introduce reinforced concrete to
Dominican construction. This was
primarily done in order to assist rapid
construction of factories and housing
following the sugar boom of the late
19th century. The sugar industry needed
happily housed employees to work in

The modern façade of the Teatro Nacional

their factories, and reinforced concrete was the cheap and easy answer. As a result, San Pedro – with the exception of the vast mansions built by the baseball elite – is probably one of the most visually unappealing cities in the country.

In the countryside, rural homes feature a number of pleasant features. They tend to be a single storey in height, are without porches and have plank siding – but they are always extremely colourful. Almost all residences are square, but the range and brightness of their colours are as arresting as the Las Vegas strip. Windows and doors in rural buildings are almost always lined up with each other in order to create alleys of air that run through the house. This serves to not only cool the structure and provide a breeze on muggy summer days, but also to protect against hurricanes. When the strong winds hit,

they move directly through the house instead of hitting doors or windows and causing damage. It's an old trick that has been used in countless Caribbean homes for centuries – and it works.

THOSE FORWARD-THINKING SPANIARDS

You might think that cities based on a grid-pattern are not all that innovative, but back in the 16th century, they were a novel idea. Up until then, European cities were constructed in a 'higgledy-piggledy' fashion. If someone needed a street built in a particular direction, then it was built with no thought taken as to the effect it would have on the city as a whole. Today, the grid-pattern is what almost every American city is based upon. It can be seen working effectively in such great metropolises as New York and Chicago.

The hustle and bustle of Avenida Duarte

Taino Indians

While the Taino Indians weren't the first people to settle in the Dominican Republic, they were the residents at the time of Columbus's discovery of the New World. Originally, Hispaniola was the home of the Carib Indians. In approximately 1 AD, the Taino sailed up from Venezuela and Colombia and forced the Caribs off the island. From that point until 1492, the Taino people lived peacefully, apart from a few minor skirmishes with natives from nearby islands.

Taino pictograms

Agriculture and fishing were the main sources of food and income for the Taino. They used tobacco for ceremonial purposes and for pleasure in the form of cigars. Religion was heavily based upon a system of ancestor worship. As such, great emphasis was placed on the role of the priest in the community.

Spirits were believed to live throughout the island, and would be marked by statues constructed from wood or stone. It is still possible to see such 'idols' today, both in their original habitat and in the various museums scattered throughout the Dominican Republic.

Contact

Contact between Europeans and the Taino was made on 6 December 1492. Columbus arrived at La Navidad, near what is now Cap Haïtien in Haiti, and established a settlement. His crew, eager to get their hands on the legendary gold that was reputed to lie in the Cordillera Central, fought amongst themselves to stay. Believing that he had successfully set the wheels in motion for a new society, Columbus returned across the ocean to report on his findings to the Spanish crown.

Revenge

In late 1493, Columbus was sent back to the New World to further tighten Spain's hold on its new possessions. Upon reaching La Navidad, he discovered that the entire settlement had been wiped out, fallen victim either to the Tainos or to disease. A second settlement called La Isabela was then founded around 100km (60 miles) further east, in present-day Dominican Republic – but the damage had been done. Relations between the Taino and Spanish were never to recover.

Over the next ten years, thousands of Spaniards were sent to the Dominican to deal with the Taino 'problem'. Columbus had seen large amounts of gold jewellery exhibited by the Taino, and he was determined to get his hands on it. Several expeditions were made into the interior in search of gold: the superior weaponry of the conquistadors ensured that they would have no problem wrenching it from the hands of the Indian population.

By 1503, an *encomienda* system was introduced, allowing each Spanish settler to cultivate a plot of land for the Spanish crown. Desperate for labour, the Europeans enslaved every Indian they could find – the Spaniards had no intention of getting their own hands dirty. At this point in time, the Taino population numbered approximately 300,000. But the conditions they were forced to live in under the Spanish quickly decimated their numbers. Imported diseases, suicide, and murder at the hands of the gold-crazy Spanish reduced that figure to 500 less than 40 years after Columbus landed on Hispaniola's northern coast. Today, there are no Dominican residents who can claim to be Taino.

Tracing Taino culture

There are a number of Taino artefacts in Dominican museums, but if you want to see remnants of the culture in natural surroundings, then it is best to travel to the remote Haitian border region, or to the southwest of the country near Barahona. Here is where you will see the finest examples of Taino hieroglyphs and cave painting. One of the best Taino archaeological sites is an enormous circle of boulders around a central slab that was once used for religious purposes, located 5km (3 miles) east of Santiago de la Cruz on Highway 18 in Los Indios de Chacuey.

Pre-Columbian statuary

Enriquillo – a Taino Legend

The history of the Taino people is a sad one, and a striking example of how negative the effects of colonialism could be. But, there is one figure who managed to give the Taino people a glimmer of hope during the harsh years of Spanish rule: Enriquillo.

The making of a revolutionary

Enriquillo was the orphan son of a Taino noble, who was educated by the Spanish at the Monasterio San Francisco, then sent to work under the colonial *repartimiento* system that forced Taino slaves to work for Spanish leaseholders. In 1519, Enriquillo escaped; he then gathered a large band of Tainos to conduct raids from his base in the south. He believed that it was better to die in battle than live under Spanish rule.

For 11 years, the Spanish desperately attempted to get rid of him. Numerous parties were sent out to assassinate him, and all failed. Hiding out in the mountainous southwest, and practising guerrilla tactics against the Spaniards, Enriquillo and his men managed to stay out of reach of their rulers.

Peace and pox

In 1530, the Spaniards finally admitted defeat and signed a peace treaty. But it was a peace that was to be short-lived. Enriquillo's band settled along the shores of what is now called Lago Enriquillo, and started to develop a Taino society that was free from the military threat they had fought against for over a decade. All seemed fine until one by one the entire community began to drop dead of smallpox – the deadly disease that had been introduced by the Europeans when they arrived in the country. Taino immune systems could not cope, and ten years later, Enriquillo's utopian community had disappeared.

A Dominican icon

Enriquillo's name and reputation were largely erased from the history books by the Spanish, until 1882, when an author and politician by the name of Manuel Jesús de Galván wrote a novel that conferred hero status on the Indian revolutionary.

Galván hailed from the elite classes of Santo Domingo, and his choice of topic was deliberate. The writer was virulently anti-African, and desperately wanted to rid the Dominican of any African influences in order to promote a more European mentality. He was a firm advocate of annexing the Dominican to Spain; he also hated merengue music and African-inspired religious practices because he felt they were too 'country'. In reality, he harboured a strong racist streak. However, the economic devastation of the 18th century had done much to encourage the mingling of the races, and even the highest Dominican classes could not claim to be

Opposite: Enriquillo – the legendary Taino hero
Above: Reproduction Taino warrior masks can be found in local shops
Right: Characteristic Taino markings in Las Caritas caves

of 'pure' blood. So Galván settled on Enriquillo as the only truly non-African Dominican hero he could write about.

The book and its effects

The book claimed to be a biography, but was largely fictionalised and quickly became a hit amongst the Dominican elite because it denied any sense of Spanish-African heritage. The higher classes were desperate to remove any traces of 'African-ness' from Dominican history, because they didn't want to give the majority mulatto population any sense of pride or power. This 'white is right' attitude is one that continues today and is reflected in the abysmal treatment of Haitian immigrants and the second-class status given to residents with darker skin tones.

One of the worst proponents of anti-African sentiment was the dictator Trujillo, who often referred to Enriquillo as a personal hero. Unsurprisingly, Trujillo's immigration policy during his time in power encouraged European settlers to move to the Dominican in an effort to 'whiten up' the population.

Santo Domingo

Founded in 1496 by Christopher Columbus's brother Bartolomé, the city of Santo Domingo is one of the oldest cities in the New World and the capital city of the Dominican Republic. Modern and gleaming, old and crumbling, buzzing with atmosphere, sleepy and sedate – the Dominican's largest metropolis is all this and more. At one point in its history, Santo Domingo could have laid claim to being the richest city in the Americas. Unfortunately, that period ended almost five centuries ago when the Spanish monarchy moved its economic bases and trading posts to the much safer ports of Havana, Lima and Cartagena.

Avenida Duarte activity

Location, location, location

The city was originally founded on the eastern bank of the Río Ozama, but quickly switched banks following the arrival of Governor Nicolás de Ovando two years later. Ovando declared that all buildings should be built out of stone – as a result the city was affected by far fewer fires than other settlements in the Caribbean (and far more authentic buildings survived from the period for tourists to enjoy today).

For almost a century, Santo Domingo served as the capital of Spanish America and as a base for Spanish exploration in the region. Cortés, Ponce de León, Velázquez and Balboa all began their epic journeys from Santo Domingo, giving the city the unofficial title of 'capital of conquests'.

First at everything

Santo Domingo's old town has been declared a UNESCO World Cultural Heritage site, in recognition of its unique place in American history. It was the first city in this region to build a cathedral, to create a monetary system, to construct a university and to develop a political system.

In many ways, a walk around the Zona Colonial (Old Town) is like a step back to the heady days of the early 16th century, when Santo Domingo was without compare and could look down its nose at all the other cities around. But all this came to a crashing end in 1562 when a huge earthquake destroyed much of the town. By this point, Spain had also discovered and developed two other colonies of greater importance – and, more importantly, with greater reserves of gold: Mexico and Peru. The arrival of Sir Frances Drake in 1586 merely served to put the final nail in Santa Domingo's coffin, as his team of privateers looted, pillaged and plundered to their heart's content.

Yesterday and today

Fast forward about 450 years and you will discover that Santo Domingo is (obviously) a much-changed place. Traffic is epic in weight, air pollution is rife and neon signs and concrete slabs have replaced the delicate stone structures that once dominated the heart of town. But the true colonial heart of this city remains. You just have to look past the sprawl, the construction and the American-style strip-malls to find what you are looking for.

Columbus's Palace is still here, lovingly cared for near the cobblestoned streets and limestone walls of the old town that his family founded and built. Listen closely and you may be able to hear the crash of conquistador armour as they embark on another mission to conquer the Americas; the sound of slaves as they sing their songs and dream of freedom, or the chatter of merchants as they load up tropical wares for sale in Spain.

Beginning your journey

As the major gateway to the Dominican, you will find that Santo Domingo is both a perfect introduction and a crashing let-down. Its major problem is that it's a city – and a thoroughly chaotic one at that. Laying claim to being the first city in the Americas may be great for the tourist guides and history books, but the actuality is a bit

The gardens of the Casa de Bastidas

disappointing. What is good about Santo Domingo, however, is its location, flavour and wealth of sights. If you want to discover beaches, develop a tropical mentality and gaze at stunning countryside, you will find all that within easy reach of the capital. But do not let your desire for sun and sand overtake you before you have a chance to explore what Santo Domingo has to offer.

Tantalising the tourists

The most visited site in the city is obviously and justifiably the Zona Colonial. The neighbourhood is surprisingly large and features dozens of old buildings, plenty of character, and a stunning setting right on the banks of the Ozama River.

Many visitors choose to limit their activity to this one section of town –

and it is easy to see why. The best boutique hotels, cafés and restaurants can all be found here, and there is plenty to keep you occupied for two to three days.

To truly experience and explore Dominican culture, however, you will have to leave this neighbourhood at some point. Three incredible museums worth taking time out to explore are the Museo del Hombre Dominicano, the Museo de Arte Moderno and the Museo Prehispánico. The Museo Prehispánico was built to preserve the remaining artefacts of Taino culture and civilisation, which predated Columbus's arrival. Conveniently, all three museums are situated on the Plaza de la Cultura, and all three can easily be visited in one day.

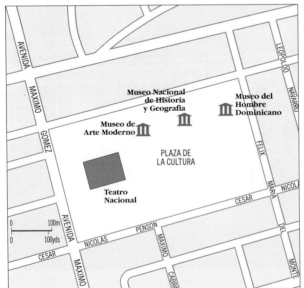

Nighttime is the right time

Santo Domingo has a thriving music scene and is one of the capitals of Latin beats. The Dominican sound is the sound of the merengue, a form of music that can trace its roots back to songs sung by African slaves. It is combined with Haitian rhythms and the passion that comes from the Dominican heart.

Club and nighttime activity is centred – as it is in most Dominican cities – around its Malecón, a beach-straddling boardwalk that seems to go on and on. The party never ends here, and it has already been dubbed the 'planet's longest disco' by *The Guinness Book of World Records*.

Go green

If ever the hustle and bustle gets to be too much, there are plenty of places to while away a few hours without having to face the choking exhaust that can sometimes seem to blanket every corner. One of the finest places for a stroll is the botanical gardens, the green lung of the city that displays plants from every corner of the country. To make the most of your time in this expansive park, look for the orchid pavilion with more than 300 examples of the fragile flower; the dainty Japanese garden, complete with pagoda and shaded benches; and the greenhouses that are dedicated to aquatic and rainforest plants and flowers.

In winter, immerse yourself in everything Dominican with a trip to the Estadio Quisqueya to witness professional baseball teams battle it out for supremacy. Anyone who has ever referred to the sport as 'America's favourite pastime' hasn't been to the Dominican. No other country lives or dies by the scoreboard as much as this one.

Top it all off with a trip to the Los Tres Ojos (Three Eyes) complex of caves, and you'll see the best this city has to offer. Paths lead to a series of three delicate lagoons that take you back to the days when the caves were used for Taino religious ceremonies.

Take time out to enjoy the tropical flowers in the botanical gardens

Walk:
Strolling down the Malecón

The pulsing, modern, sun-drenched heart of Santo Domingo lies on its famous Malecón boardwalk. Brash, barmy and beautiful, it dances day and night to a beat all its own. This stroll is approximately 6km (3.75 miles) long, and how long it takes will depend on how many stops you make. Do it by day to see the sights or by night to enjoy the music and people-watching.

Allow: 6–7 hours. Begin at the industrial port at the mouth of the Río Ozama, where Avenida George Washington starts.

1 City wall and San José Fort

At the start of the Malecón is an intact 100m section of the city's old walls. The 17th-century San José Fort lies next to it, and was originally built to defend the city from attempted invasion after the British tried to seize the city in 1635. Cannons point across the street in the direction of the statue of Fray Montesino, a Catholic priest who lived in the Dominican in its early days and preached against the harsh treatment of the Taino Indians.

This section of the boardwalk is the most popular, especially at night.

Live music and outdoor concerts on weekends draw massive crowds from all walks of life. Savour the atmosphere by sitting down and enjoying a light meal at La Parrillada, an outdoor restaurant that always draws a lively crowd.

Walk 1km (just over half a mile) west along Avenida George Washington (The Malecón) until you reach La Obeliska.

2 La Obeliska

The dictator Rafael Trujillo (ruled 1930–61) placed this obelisk on Avenida George Washington in 1941 to commemorate the repayment of a large debt to the United States. The large, two-pronged monument is not especially loved by locals.

Continue walking southwest a further 1km (half a mile) to reach El Obelisco.

3 El Obelisco

The dictator Trujillo was certainly fond of his obelisks. This one commemorates the rechristening of the city as Ciudad Trujillo in 1936. (The name did not last very long.) Today, the obelisk is decidedly anti-Trujillo in sentiment, and bears a number of murals honouring the Mirabel sisters – national martyrs who were gunned down by Trujillo's forces after they visited their husbands in prison. *Continue walking southwest.*

4 The outdoor party zones

The next 4km (2.5 miles) of boardwalk run past high-rise hotels, outdoor restaurants and shops, worth exploring if you have the time. By night this section becomes a giant outdoor disco, thanks to legal outdoor party zones that allow dancers on the street – especially near the avenidas Sánchez and Máximo Gómez. Join in the fun by kicking up your heels and grabbing a drink from one of the street-side salesmen. *Continue southwest to the Centro de los Héroes.*

5 Centro de los Héroes

This is the administrative headquarters of the country and has a decidedly monumental look to it. A globe and a large pink arch span the road here. It's worth stopping to take a look at the architecture.

At the far western edge of the square is the Teatro de Agua y Luz, an outdoor amphitheatre with colourful fountains and light displays.

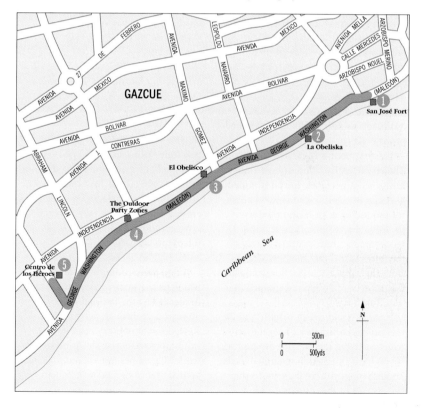

The Museums of the Plaza de la Cultura

Near the centre of the city, on land once owned by the dictator Trujillo, is a complex of museums set in lush, green surroundings. Trujillo donated the land following his assassination in 1961 in order to further exploration of Dominican culture. The result is four museums and a national theatre. All of the museums are closed on Mondays and public holidays. Disappointingly, information signs and displays are in Spanish only.

The Teatro Nacional
(National Theatre)

Museo Nacional de Historia Natural

The Museum of Natural History is fascinating if you have an interest in the topography and natural past of the country. However, the descriptions are all in Spanish so, without at least a basic knowledge of the language, you will find it difficult to gain a full understanding of the exhibits.

The first floor is dedicated to amber. There is an explanation of how amber forms, its importance, how it is mined, and why the Dominican is well known for producing it. In relation to this there is a discussion of the region's biogeographic history and a survey of the information that has been drawn from the various insects, flora and fauna that have been discovered trapped in island amber.

Floor two focuses on wildlife and the various microclimate and vegetation zones scattered throughout the country. If you have an aversion to stuffed birds and fish, then you might want to skip this section of the museum. The third floor is dedicated to endemic Dominican species – once again stuffed and displayed.

Museo Nacional de Historia Natural, Plaza de la Cultura. Tel: (809) 689 0106. Open: 10am–5pm Tues–Sun. Admission fee.

Museo de Arte Moderno

If you think that Dominican art is all about primitive art or art naïf, then this museum will do much to change your mind. The Museum of Modern Art was created to promote the Dominican artists of today, and to challenge international views of Caribbean culture and design in general.

A tour from room to room will take you from the work of Dominican artists influenced by the Parisian movement of 50 years ago, through permanent collections, temporary exhibits and exhibitions of local and Caribbean works. Big names to look out for during your visit include José Vela Zanetti, Jaime Colson, Candido Bidó, Martín

Santos, Adriana Billini, Dario Suro and Celeste Woss y Gil.

Modern Dominican art draws from many themes, but Taino art, and *campesino* issues of poverty and mythology, are certainly prevalent. Look at Taino pottery shards and rock paintings in other parts of the country, and you may spot a repeated symbol or two in the works hung here.

Museo de Arte Moderno, Plaza de la Cultura. Tel: (809) 685 2153. Open: 10am–5pm Tues–Sun. Admission fee.

Museo Nacional de Historia y Geografia

Located next to the modern art museum, the museum of history and geography is a collection of Dominican historical memorabilia from the past two centuries. The first floor features an adequate collection of Taino sculptures, but the truly good stuff is up on the second floor. The Haitian occupation, the American occupation of 1916 and the Trujillo dictatorship are all covered here in fascinating (and sometimes horrifying) detail.

The Haitian occupation exhibit is the weakest of the three; it has examples of weapons from the period and patriotic art. The American exhibit features propaganda from the period as well as examples of military uniforms of the day. There is even an electric chair that was once used to murder Dominican prisoners. A photograph hanging above the chair depicts one of the actual

The gardens around the Museo de Arte Moderno

victims. Guerrillas used this photograph to convince Dominicans to join their efforts to kick the American forces out.

The coverage of Trujillo's years is the most shocking of all, with hundreds of artefacts depicting the grotesque wealth and power enjoyed by the dictator while the country was starving around him. Marvel at the gold and ivory personal effects, military uniform and presidential sash, as well as the pancake makeup he used to hide his darker skin tones. Even more shocking are the 'El Benefactor' signs posted in every home and above every public place, thanking the dictator for his generosity, and the ID cards that all citizens were forced to carry: these listed their identity by number and not name. In the centre of the room is a bullet-riddled automobile that was part of his presidential motorcade on the day he was shot in 1961.

Museo de Historia y Geografía, Plaza de la Cultura. Tel: (809) 686 6668. Open: 9.30am–5pm Tues–Sun. Admission fee.

A sculptural fountain at the Museo de Arte Moderno

Museo del Hombre Dominicano

Most interesting of all the museums in the plaza is the Museum of Dominican Man. This extraordinary collection of Taino artefacts and historical information about Hispaniola's pre-Columbian people is the most extensive on the island, and – for those with an interest in the country's past – should be considered a 'must-see' stop. Exhibits range from displays outlining tools the Taino used and items they left behind on their travels, through to stone obelisks and reconstructions of burial mounds.

The first two floors can be missed: the ground floor is mostly taken up by a massive gift shop and the first is closed to the public. Floor two is where the action begins, with a large room containing displays of Taino sculpture, gods, hatchets and spearheads. The far end of the room features elaborate jewellery with intricate markings made from conch shell, tooth, coral and stone. There is also a case filled with gruesome death heads and a few examples of artwork produced by Taino ancestors during the period when they lived in the Amazon basin.

The fourth floor is dedicated to Dominican culture after Columbus, with – for the Dominicans – a very untypical emphasis on African culture. The first room discusses the impact of the slave trade on the country, visually examining the difference between African peasants and Dominican *campesinos* (farmers).

Do not miss the reconstruction of the 'typical' country house: it will give you a good idea of the simplicity of peasant

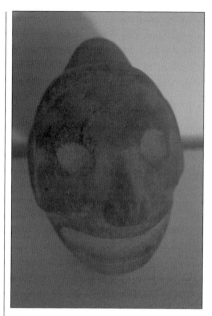

Taino treasure

life in the country. This is followed by an absolutely fantastic look at the syncretic religion and practices in the country, and the effects slavery and Haiti have had on Dominican Catholicism. This room features stunning photographs of rural fiestas and a Dominican voodoo altar. Note the use of Catholic iconography and the sacrificial use of cigarettes, a chicken and a bottle of rum.

Further displays exhibit collections of local musical instruments and three large cases depicting carnival celebrations in Santo Domingo, Monte Cristi and La Vega.

Museo del Hombre Dominicano, Plaza de la Cultura. Tel: (809) 687 3622. Open: 10am–5pm Tues–Sun. Admission fee.

Zona Colonial

Constituting just one per cent of the total area of Santo Domingo, the Zona Colonial is but a tiny neighbourhood in a sea of urbanity – but what a neighbourhood it is. The typical first port of call for all visitors to the capital, the Zona Colonial (or Old Town) has really come into its own since interest in the Dominican's past blossomed in the 1960s. While some of the buildings date back to the 16th century, the bulk of them are more modern reconstructions, thanks to Sir Frances Drake. In 1586, Drake sacked the city and left it to burn. This began a long period of decline for the city, as pirates, earthquakes, hurricanes and fires combined to tear Santo Domingo apart.

Inside the Catedral Basílica Menor de Santa Maria

Getting your bearings

The oldest paved road in the Americas is Calle Las Damas, situated immediately adjacent to the Fortress. The street got its name thanks to the propensity of the ladies of the court to take their evening promenade down its length. In keeping with the Spanish colonial feel, the Calle remains cobblestoned; it also features gas lighting instead of electric to give it a bit of authenticity.

You can navigate by following Calle El Conde, which runs the length of the old city from the entrance gate. This street pretty much cuts directly through the centre of the district – if you can find it you will know exactly where you are. This is also the best path to take if you want to get to Puerte El Conde, the Fortaleza Ozama or the river. The entire stretch is pedestrianised, so you won't have to worry about Santo's crazy drivers at any time. It's a pleasant place to stroll and window-shop: there are plenty of cafés, boutiques and bars along the route.

Most street names in the city will be familiar to you if you know anything about Dominican history, as they are all named after freedom-fighters and those leaders who played a strong role in ensuring that the nation became independent from Spain.

The fortress

In 1502, Spain knew that Holland, France and England would be very keen to gain possessions in the New World. The Spanish therefore decided to fortify the city by constructing a tower to guard the port. City walls were built later, in 1543, by the architect Roderigo de Liendo. Today, these walls have only been partly restored.

If you want to see a good section to get an idea of what they looked like, head to the beginning of the Avenida George Washington. Twenty defensive positions were built along the walls, of which six were access gates to the city. The rest were forts or bastions reserved for military purposes. The largest fort of them all was the Fortaleza Ozama (or Fortaleza Santo Domingo as it is more commonly known), built near the mouth of the Río Ozama on the Avenida del Puerto. Fortaleza Santo Domingo is the oldest fort in America, and was constructed between 1503 and 1507.

The architect's house is located just to the north, and is currently being restored in order to transform it into a boutique hotel. The fort functioned as a military base for more than 450 years, and was decommissioned as recently as 1965, following the American invasion.

It was from this building that the Spanish launched a number of missions, including their conquests of Jamaica, Cuba, Columbia, Peru and Mexico.

Inside the main neo-Classical gate is a courtyard with a statue of González Oveido, commander of the fort from 1533 to 1557 and author of the first *History of the Indies*. The largest structure in the complex is the Torre de Homenaje (Tower of Homage), a Medieval-style tower located in the most impenetrable part of the fortress and used for centuries as a prison. The top of the tower features incredible views of the entire Zona. Note the hole in the floor through which prisoners were once dropped into their cells.

The Santa Maria cathedral was Santo Domingo's first Catholic church

Walk: Santo Domingo's ancient heart

A walk around the Zona Colonial is a walk around the history of the Dominican Republic and Spanish colonialism. Begin your journey at the Fortaleza Santo Domingo. Truly a tour not to be missed!

Allow: 6–8 hours, depending on stops. This journey looks a lot longer than it is: as the Zona Colonial is so compact, the amount of walking is limited.

1 The Fortaleza Santo Domingo

(see p51)
Walk west to the Catedral Basílica Menor de Santa Maria.

2 The Catedral

The Catedral Basílica Menor de Santa Maria was the first cathedral in the Americas. Construction began in 1514 when the first stone was laid by the son of Christopher Columbus, Diego Colón. In 1540, work on the building ground to a halt due to a lack of funds. A steeple and bell tower that were included in the architect's original plans were never actually completed.

Unfortunately, little remains of the original interior decor. Sir Francis Drake used the cathedral as his headquarters during his rape of the city in 1586. His men removed everything they could, and unfortunately all of it has been lost. In 1877, restoration uncovered the remains of a 16th-century man whom many assumed to be Christopher Columbus. It was probably not him, but you would be well advised not to cast any doubt on this belief: it is a source of

pride to the Dominicans. Full restoration of the entire cathedral was completed in 1992 to coincide with the 500th anniversary of the arrival of Columbus. The windows, doors and altars have all been returned to their original magnificence.

Catedral Basílica Menor de Santa Maria, Entrance facing Parque Colón. No phone. Open: daily 9am–4pm. Free. (No shorts are permitted. Women may be asked to wear skirts, not trousers.)
Cross to the park on the north side of the cathedral next to Calle El Conde.

3 Parque Colón

A gracious park, Parque Colón is centred around a statue of Christopher Columbus. Beneath him Taino women worship at his feet in a depiction that nowadays seems highly politically incorrect. The trees were badly damaged during Hurricane Georges in 1998.

The park is a nice place in which to sit and enjoy a cool drink.
Walk towards Calle El Conde and cross the street.

4 Museo de Ambar

A simple museum that acts more as a gift shop than as an effective exploration of Dominican amber. The museum opened in 1998 and does a good trade in jewellery crafted on the island. The benefit of shopping here is that you know that what you're getting is the real thing. However, be warned: black coral is sold here. This is an item that is protected by CITES and will not be permitted in your home country.
Museo de Ambar, Parque Colón. Tel: (809) 221 1333. Open: 9am–5pm. Admission fee.
Walk towards the east side of the plaza.

5 Palacio de Borgella

A beautiful 19th-century 'palace' built by Haitians during the French occupation. Note the brick arcades on the ground floor. Trolley buses stop immediately outside the entrance if you prefer to tour the Colonial Zone using four wheels and a guide.
Continue to Calle de Las Damas.

6 Calle de Las Damas

Running north from the Fortaleza is the Calle de Las Damas, the oldest paved street in the New World. There are dozens of buildings of historical interest lining this strip, so be selective about

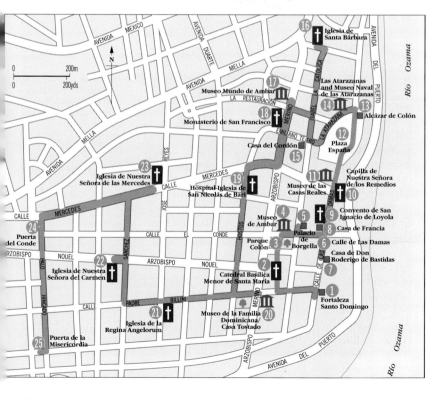

which ones you want to go into if you don't want to spend the whole day here. *Go south to the Casa de Don Roderigo de Bastidas.*

7 Casa de Don Roderigo de Bastidas
You will come across the glorious Casa de Don Roderigo almost as soon as you enter the Calle de Las Damas. This beautiful home was constructed in 1510, built right into the city walls. This was the house of the royal tax collector and mayor. He eventually went on to colonise Colombia. The home is large

and built in the traditional Spanish style of the time, with a courtyard lined with arches around all four walls.
Casa de Don Roderigo de Bastidas, Calle de Las Damas. Open: 9.30am–5pm Mon–Fri. Free.
Go back north along the Calle de Las Damas.

8 Casa de Francia
Located opposite the Hostal Nicolás de Ovando is the Casa de Francia. Currently home to the French Embassy cultural division, this structure can

Lighting your way in the Zona Colonial

Leather goods adorn the market stalls

boast a number of famous former occupants, including Hernán Cortés. This is allegedly the building where he planned his infamous campaign to capture Mexico.

Casa de Francia, Calle de Las Damas 42. Tel: (809) 685 0840. Open: 9am–5pm Mon–Fri. Free.
Continue next door.

9 Convento de San Ignacio de Loyola

An 18th-century Jesuit monastery and church. Since 1958, this building has functioned as the National Pantheon. Trujillo restored the church in 1955, adding tons of marble and tombs or memorials to honour national heroes. Look for the elaborate tomb Trujillo built for himself with the title 'Benefactor of the Fatherland'. After his assassination, he was never given the honour of being laid to rest in it. Now it serves simply as a monument to his ostentation.

Convento de San Ignacio de Loyola, Calle de Las Damas between Mercedes and El Conde. Tel: (809) 682 0185. Open: 9am–5pm Tues–Sun. Free.
Cross the street.

10 Capilla de Nuestra Señora de los Remedios

A private chapel built by the Dávila family in the early 16th century. Next to it is a sundial, constructed in 1753 so that court officials could tell the time by looking out of their window.

Capilla de Nuestra Señora de los Remedios, Corner of Las Damas and Mercedes. Irregular hours. Free.
Continue up Calle de Las Damas.

11 Museo de las Casas Reales

A reconstructed 16th-century building, this was once the Palace of the Governors and Captains-General, and of the Real Audiencia and Chancery of the Indies. The most notable feature is the door, typical of its time. The Real Audiencia was the Dominican supreme court, composed of three judges and put in place to keep the power of the governor in check. Its legal power extended throughout the Caribbean, right to the mainland coast.

Today, it is a wonderful colonial museum. Among its exhibits are samples of booty dredged up from ships sunk in regional waters.

Museo de las Casas Reales, Calle de Las Damas. Tel: (809) 682 4202. Open: 9am–6pm Tues–Sun. Admission fee.
Walk to the end of Calle de Las Damas.

12 Plaza España

An open park surrounded by monuments. The statue that stands in the centre is of Nicolás de Ovando, one of the chief architects of the city. There are beautiful views over the river and numerous cafés in which to stop for a drink or a light meal.

Night brings cultural events to the square, including live music, folk dancing and street theatre.

Wander over to the corner of Las Damas and Emiliano Tejera.

13 Alcázar de Colón

The Alcázar was the home of the first viceroy, Diego Colón. It was built between 1510 and 1514 to house his court and wife, and was constructed without the use of any nails! This was

Shop for unusual souvenirs in the *mercado* (market)

A treasure trove of trinkets

the seat and symbol of the Spanish Crown in the New World until the Colón family returned to Spain in 1577. The home was sacked by Drake in 1586 and left to fall into ruin, until it was finally abandoned in 1770.

Attempts were later made to use it as a jail, but collapses in the underlying structure of the building in 1809 and 1835 meant that it became little more than a pile of unstable timber. In 1957, restoration began when specialist stone-masons were brought in to survey the damage. Today, it has been completely restored to its former glory.

An interesting museum of religious and colonial art and artefacts is housed within its walls.
Alcázar de Colón, Corner of Calle de Las Damas and Emiliano Tejera. No phone. Open: 9am–5pm daily. Admission fee. Head towards the dockyards next to the Alcázar.

14 Las Atarazanas and the Museo Naval de las Atarazanas

Las Atarazanas are a group of 16th-century buildings that once housed warehouses, taverns and an arsenal. The entire complex has now been transformed into a chic, tourist-oriented collection of shops and restaurants.

A museum at the end of the complex houses recovered treasure from a number of shipwrecks, in addition to accounts of the attempts made to raise the 17th- and 18th-century ships that currently lie off the coast of the Dominican.
Museo Naval de las Atarazanas, Las Atarazanas. Tel: (809) 682 5834. Open: daily 9am–6pm. Admission: Free.

Return to Calle Emiliano Tejero and walk inland until you reach the junction with Isabel La Católica. Your next stop will be on the southwest corner.

15 Casa del Cordón

Francisco de Garay was a sailor and expeditioner who accompanied Columbus on his first voyage to Hispaniola in 1492. The Casa del Cordón was built by De Garay in 1509 as a tribute to Columbus. It was named for the cord of the Franciscan Order, in honour of the occasion in 1497 when the famed explorer dressed in a Franciscan habit to be received by the Catholic kings at the Casa del Cordón in Burgos, Spain. Take a peek above the door to see what the cord looks like. In its early days, the building was used as a court house. It is now a Banco Popular.
Casa del Cordón, Calle Emiliano Tejeres. No phone. Free guided tours during regular office hours. Continue north up Isabel La Católica.

16 Iglesia de Santa Bárbara

The only joint church and fort in Santo Domingo. Built in 1574, the church was constructed on the site of the city quarry, in honour of the patron saint of the military. A hurricane destroyed the church in 1591; however, the city reconstructed it at the beginning of the 17th century. As such, it combines a wide range of styles from both periods.
Go back down Isabel La Católica until you reach La Restauración and go west. Turn right at the next crossroads and your next stop will be on the immediate left.

17 Museo Mundo de Ambar

Much better than the first amber museum on the tour, this collection features hundreds of insects, butterflies and plantlife trapped in amber, some of which are millions of years old. Staff are very knowledgeable and will give you invaluable tips on how you can distinguish the real stuff from the fake.

Mundo de Ambar, Calle Arzobispo Meriño 452. Tel: (809) 682 3309. Open: 9am–4pm daily. Admission fee.
Return to Restauración and continue west until you reach Calle Hostos. Turn left. The next stop is on the right.

18 Monasterio de San Francisco

The Monasterio de San Francisco is the first monastery in America, built some time during the first half of the 16th century. The exterior decoration very much follows the tastes of the time, with an Isabelline monastery entrance and Franciscan cord and a crest for illustration. The façade at the west end of the church was constructed after the rest of the building was complete, and features the sober classicism favoured by Philip II post-1570.

The monastery (like almost everything else in the Zona Colonial) was sacked by Drake in 1586 and destroyed by earthquakes in 1673 and 1751. However, it was rebuilt each time. From 1880–1930, the complex was used as an asylum to house the insane. See if you can spot the metal brackets attached to floors and walls from which patients were restrained with chains. Today, the monastery is used primarily for cultural events.

Monasterio de San Francisco, Corner of Hostos between Emiliano Tejera and Restauración. No phone. Open: 9am–5pm daily. Free. Continue south on Hostos until you pass Calle Mercedes. Your next stop will be on the right.

19 Hospital-Iglesia de San Nicolás de Bari

Yet another first: this time it is the first permanent hospital built in America. Construction began in 1509 and continued for almost 50 years, until it was finally completed in 1552. Two-storey wings held the sick, while a small church was used for worship. Probably the best-constructed building from its time in all of Santo Domingo, it survived numerous hurricanes, fires, floods and earthquakes – until 1911, when some of its walls were knocked down.

Keep going south on Hostos until you reach Calle Padre Billini. Turn left after one block and look to your right after you cross over at the next junction to reach your next stop.

20 Museo de la Familia Dominicana

A museum housing a collection of 19th-century furniture and antiques in an early 16th-century mansion. The house was once home of the writer Francisco de Tostado.

Museo de la Familia Dominicana, Corner of Padre Billini and Arzobispo Meriño. Tel: (809) 689 5057. Open: daily 9am–5pm. Admission fee.
Backtrack west along Padre Billini.

21 Iglesia de la Regina Angelorum

The first church built for Dominican nuns. It took almost a century to complete. One of the altars is notable for containing an entire wall of 18th-century Baroque silver.

Continue west on Padre Billini and take the next right onto Sanchez. Your next stop is on the left.

22 Iglesia de Nuestra Señora del Carmen

This 16th-century church was once the secret meeting place for revolutionaries during the fight for independence. The building is a focal point on Ash Wednesday and during Holy Week, when a 16th-century wooden sculpture of Christ becomes the centre of the city's attention.

Walk two blocks north until you reach Mercedes. Turn right, and the next church is on the corner of José Reyes.

23 Iglesia de Nuestra Señora de las Mercedes

A Gothic church with Renaissance detailing, the Iglesia de Nuestra Señora dates from 1555 and is notable for having once housed the playwright Tirso de Molina (creator of Don Juan) for two years. Molina was sent to Santo Domingo in 1616 on an official visit to teach courses in theology.

Iglesia de Nuestra Señora de las Mercedes, Corner of Las Mercedes and José Reyes. No phone. Open: irregular hours. Free. Backtrack west along Mercedes for four blocks and your next stop will be directly in front of you.

24 Puerta del Conde

The Puerta del Conde (Gate of the Count) was one of six gates leading into the city through the city walls and was named to honour Bernardo de Meneses

y Bracamonte, the Count of Peñalba. The Count was famous for having led the successful defence of 1655 against a vast invading force of more than 13,000 British troops. It also has strong resonances in terms of Dominican pride and history, for it is on this spot that – in February 1844 – a group of Dominicans stood up to the Haitian leadership and executed a bloodless coup. This action is what resulted in the establishment of an independent Dominican Republic. The very first Dominican flag was therefore raised above this gate.

Just to the west of the gate you will see a mausoleum containing the remains of three of the country's most respected heroes: Ramón Matías Mella, Juan Pablo Duarte and Francisco del Rosario Sánchez.

Turn left onto Palo Hincado before you go through the gates and go south for four blocks. Your final stop of this tour is on the right.

25 Puerta de la Misericordia

The Puerta de la Misericordia (Gate of Mercy) was once the main point of entry from the west for people wishing to enter Santo Domingo. It was built in the 16th century but didn't obtain its name until 1842, following a devastating earthquake. In order to tend for the injured and homeless, a large tent city was erected next to the gate to provide shelter and warmth. The gate became known as 'merciful'.

From this point you can either leave the Zona Colonial and return to your hotel or enjoy a further stroll along the pedestrianised shopping and dining street, Calle El Conde.

Boca Chica

The town of Boca Chica is one of the Dominican's most popular beach resorts, thanks largely to the fact that it is located a mere 25km (15.5 miles) east of the capital city. Once one of the most beautiful and exclusive spots in which to enjoy a swim in the Dominican, things have taken a turn for the scandalous lately, with dozens of 'short-term' hotels and freelance guides now on offer.

The perfect *playa* at Boca Chica

While the people and hotels of Boca Chica have rapidly become rather seedy, it has to be said that the physical surroundings of the community remain superb, situated as it is along a small bay protected by shoals.

Weekends are especially wild: city-slickers from Santo Domingo make a habit of piling into their cars to make the quick journey to Boca Chica in order to enjoy the crystal-blue waters of the Caribbean and soak up the sun.

Taino treasure

Before all the parties and prostitution, the region of Boca Chica was a major centre for the Taino civilisation. It was so important that archaeologists and anthropologists often refer to Taino treasures discovered along this stretch of the island (from San Cristóbal to Macao) as hailing from the 'Chicoid Culture'. Following colonisation, the town lost this prominence, and functioned primarily as a sleepy sugar-mill town until the Trujillo era brought the elite class to its beaches to enjoy privacy and parties away from the glare of the capital (yet still within striking distance of its trappings).

Getting around

Boca Chica is relatively compact, occupying a 10-by-15-block area between Carretera 3 and Bahía de Andrés. From the Carretera, there are three main streets that lead down to the beach: Avenidas 24 de Julio, Caracol and Bautista Vicini. From here it is an easy drive to the seaside arteries of Avenidas Duarte or San Rafael.

Like most Dominican towns, Boca Chica thankfully follows a grid pattern and is very easy to negotiate. There are no one-way systems to worry about so, as long as you know which direction you're trying to go in, you should eventually find your way there. If in doubt, keep going south from the Carretera and you will eventually hit the beach at some point along its golden stretch.

There is a distinct slope from the highway to the sea that can sometimes challenge the physically unfit. The further away from Avenida Duarte that you find yourself, the more you are going to experience a bit of physical exertion when you attempt to get back to your hotel room at the end of the day. It is for this reason that three-quarters

A serenade, perhaps?

of the population – both native and non- – can be found near the beach at Avenida Duarte at all times throughout the day, while the rest of the town often resembles a ghost town.

Today's tourism

Following the rise in international interest in the Dominican Republic that began in the early 1970s, Boca Chica became a major tourism destination. In its early days, the town was considered quite exclusive, and often saw its fair share of Hollywood celebrities and noted politicians. Its decline in popularity began as other parts of the country began developing all-inclusive resort communities, leaving Boca Chica – with its limited accommodation options – to lag behind.

By far the most visited attraction (and the reason for Boca Chica's existence) is the beach. The waters tend to remain

The 'corner shop' comes to the beach

low, so seem made for families and swimmers looking for a spot of relaxation. Thanks to the Caribbean's placid nature in these parts, it is often possible to walk out to the bird-inhabited mangrove island of La Matica, located just offshore. The beach is wide and lined with coconut palms, behind which are numerous bars, restaurants, and shops selling typical souvenirs and swimming gear. The shallowest stretch of the playa is the Bahía de Andrés, south of Avenida San Rafael and Avenida Duarte, which is therefore quite popular with families.

No matter where you decide to place your towel, however, you will have to prepare yourself for endless pumping music. This is not a place for serenity and seclusion – especially if you're a male Westerner travelling alone, in which case you will be approached throughout the day with offers of everything from girls to drugs. Needless to say this is all highly illegal, and can turn out to be quite an annoyance if you let it.

The Playa is technically one long beach, but it does have three distinct sections. The eastern end is blocked off from the public by the Coral Hamaca Beach Hotel & Casino. Needless to say, this isn't exactly appreciated by the locals, who view this action as yet another example of being made to feel like 'second-class citizens' in their own country – and they have a point. Dominican law states that all beaches are open to the public. This law is frequently ignored, however, and – in some cases – the police support the resorts thanks to a bit of financial 'assistance'. On Coral Hamaca they have gone so far as to wall off the beach, check identification, and post armed guards to dissuade anyone from using 'their' sand. You are technically within your rights to demand access, but it is obviously not worth risking getting shot in order to make a point.

Go a few hundred metres west of the wall and you will come to the point where Calle Hungria ends. This is the main tourist beach and features dozens of establishments designed to cater to lobster-red Westerners and their Dominican counterparts.

The last segment of the beach is even more local in flavour, and can be found even further west, past a dirt parking lot where the tourist stalls drop off in favour of cheap, local food shacks. This spot is a bit muddy in terms of water quality, but it is well known as the place of choice for Dominican families. For this reason, the atmosphere here tends to be a little less wild and more safety-conscious.

Parque Nacional Submarino La Caleta

If you are a fan of wrecks and/or have always wanted to explore one, it is important to note that Boca Chica acts as an unofficial gateway to the Parque Nacional Submarino La Caleta. The national park is an offshore, protected coral reef that was formed in 1984 when the 39m (128ft) long vessel, *The Hickory*, was scuttled in these waters.

The Hickory was used as recently as the late 1970s to recover artefacts from two 18th-century ships that sank in the Bahia de Samaná during a hurricane on 25 August 1724 – the *Nuestra Señora de Guadalupe* and *El Conde de Tolosa*. Over 600 passengers were either killed by the surging waters or eaten by sharks following the incident. Work began in earnest to bring the artefacts from these two ships up from the bottom of the sea in October 1976. The captain of *The Hickory*, Tracy Bowden, and his crew, spent the next two years painstakingly recovering hundreds of pieces of jewellery, glass, silver and coin from the wrecks. These items can now be seen in the Museo de las Atarazanas in Santo Domingo's Zona Colonial.

Today, *The Hickory* is slowly being transformed into a coral reef, rusting under the Caribbean for all to admire. If you decide to explore the ship, be sure to get right down to the hull. It is well worth the effort: a peek through the portholes gives a great glimpse at the underwater life inside.

Topping up the tan on the beach

San Pedro de Macoris

While San Pedro de Macoris is a large, industrial centre in the Dominican Republic, it isn't really regarded as a town that has much to interest tourists. This is a working city for working people, and is rarely visited by those without a reason to stop. The region made its name and fortunes thanks to the vast number of sugar plantations that surround the city. As such, the economy lives and dies according to the state of the world sugar prices.

San Pedro de Macoris: a city dependent on sugar

Badly hit by Hurricane Georges in 1988, more than a third of the inhabitants of San Pedro de Macoris were made homeless following the devastating natural disaster. Unfortunately, the city's predominantly working-class population prevent most governments from caring about what happens here. Evidently the political parties cannot gain financially from this sort of place, and so the cultural and political elite largely stay well away. As a result the dock workers and inhabitants tend to be the most virulently anti-political and anti-globalisation in the country. This is a town that wears its heart on its sleeve.

Cultural influences

The cultural mix of San Pedro is a little stronger than in other pockets of the Dominican, thanks to the fact that a relatively large segment of the population hail originally from the Leeward and Windward Islands. Many of these residents have English surnames and arrived in the country in 1880 at the same time as the British – so don't be surprised if you hear someone called Johnson speaking fluent, unaccented Spanish.

These sugar-cane labourers were known as *cocolos*, due to a misinterpretation of the English name of the place from which they came: Tortola. The locals thought they came from '*Cocola*' and as a result referred to them as *cocolos*. Initially these workers would return to their home islands after the sugar-cane harvesting season, but after a while they established roots in the Dominican, and are now a valuable part of San Pedro society.

The cricket teams that these workers formed slowly developed over time into baseball teams. These are now sponsored by the individual sugar mills. Baseball battles between the mills are strongly supported, and almost every member of the population turns out to watch them on game days.

Festivals and fun

The *cocolo* population bring a number of intriguing carnival traditions to San Pedro, particularly on St Peter's Day on 29 June. On this day, the *cocolos* perform dances called *guloyas* and *momise*, which can trace their roots to the English Mummer tradition. There are also masked dance-dramas known as *la danza salvaje* (the wild dance), *la danza del Padre invierno* (dance of Father Winter, which is based on the George and the Dragon legend) and *la danza de El Codril*.

The performance skills of the *cocolo* population are highly respected and admired. Every year artists from the community are invited to display their vocal talents at the Santo Domingo carnival in February, and to sing a regional song in English and Spanish to an appreciative audience.

San Pedro flavour

San Pedro's architecture and civic monuments are largely Victorian in design. This was the period when the city saw its greatest explosion in development, when its fortunes were on the increase. The collapse of sugar prices in the late 1970s had a devastating effect on this once-proud town. This is a powerful example of how global forces affect Dominican life.

An initial glance at the smokestacks and decrepit harbour may put you off exploring the city. In addition, the sprawling slums that surround the downtown are off-putting, to say the least. But if you are looking for a true slice of working-class Dominican society that goes beyond the beach, then this city is worth putting on your list of sightseeing stops.

Not the latest mode of transport, but an effective one

Walk: Simply San Pedro

Due to the fact that the city rarely hosts any tourists, its residents are some of the friendliest in the Dominican Republic. San Pedrans are proud of their town and will go out of the way to help you make the most of it. So put on some comfortable walking shoes and prepare yourself for a journey deep into the heart of the Dominican's working-class communities. It's an eye-opening experience.

Allow: 3 hours (depending on stops). While crime rates in San Pedro are equivalent to the rest of the country, the city is quite poverty-stricken. Because of this, it is wise to keep your valuables safely locked back in your hotel room to avoid any unnecessary problems.

This walk starts at the Malecón in front of the Howard Johnson Hotel Macorix.

The striking Iglesia San Pedro Apostol

1 The Malecón

Compared to the seafront of Santo Domingo, the Malecón does not seem much to write home about – however, this is a boardwalk made and loved by the people. There are public beaches at either end; the industrial nature of the town should dissuade you from entering the water. On nights and weekends locals gather here in their finery to gossip, or watch the world go by.

Go north from the Malecón on Avenida Charro, located to the right of the Howard Johnson as you face the hotel from the boardwalk. Walk approximately 10 blocks until you reach your next stop on the left side of the street.

2 Centro Cultural 'Fermoselle'

San Pedro's former port authority is now renovated and has rotating exhibits

of local artists and old photographs.
*Centro Cultural 'Fermoselle', Corner of
Charro and 10 de Septiembre. No phone.
Open daily: 9.30am–noon & 2–5pm. Free.
Go northwest on Avenida Charro for four
more blocks. The next stop is on the right.*

3 Iglesia San Pedro Apostol
This lovely, whitewashed church was
built in 1911 and features a beautiful
mahogany altar and striking bell tower.
*Iglesia San Pedro Apostol, Corner of
Charro and Independencia.
Take the next right turn past the church,
off Charro onto Calle Duarte. Continue
until you reach the Parque Central.*

4 Parque Central
It might not look much, but it is worth
stopping by here on Monday evenings
to see *cocolo* bands perform.

Continue east past the park on Duarte.

5 The fire station
Probably one of the most intriguing
buildings in San Pedro, the fire station
is a cast-iron edifice built in 1903. Ask
nicely and they may let you go up the
circular staircase to enjoy some stunning
views of the city.
*The fire station, Calle Duarte 46.
Continue east on Avenida 27 de Febrero
and look for the coral-coloured mansion
on the right side of the street.*

6 George Bell Mansion
This ostentatious castle-style mansion
was built for the great baseball star
George Bell. Born in 1959, he became
one of the American League's biggest
hitters. This is a truly Dominican rags-
to-riches story (*see pp70–1*).

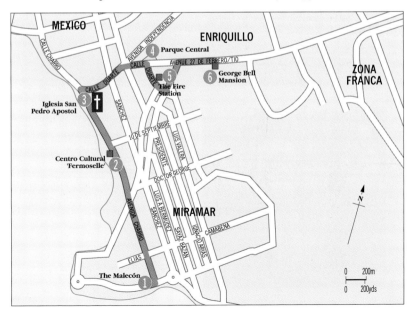

The city of San Pedro is addicted to baseball. In every street you will see children playing, old men debating the qualities of their favourite players, and teenage girls practising cheers.

George Bell, Tony Fernandez and Manny Alexander are just some of the greats who call San Pedro de Macoris home. But, what makes this city so focused around 'America's favourite pastime?' In one word – desperation.

Cultural roots

The *cocolo* immigrants imported cricket to the island in the 1880s; the American invasion of the early 20th century slowly changed the way cricket was played, and it developed into a sport based on the principles of baseball. From there, the game exploded in popularity. As the sugar mills closed down around them, the residents of San Pedro turned to baseball as a way of escaping from problems and as a means of restoring

a sense of pride. Teams composed of employees of the sugar mills became more and more competitive. By the 1970s, anyone with any talent was picking up a bat in the hope of attracting the big leagues. In one magical case, a player turned – almost overnight – from a dollar-a-day shoeshine boy to a multimillionaire. His name? Sammy Sosa.

Stats of the streets

If you arrive in San Pedro from Santo Domingo, a sign will greet you stating: 'Welcome to San Pedro de Macorís: the city that has given the most major leaguers to the world.' There are currently more than 60 Dominicans in the major leagues – the equivalent of about three full teams … and then there are the minor leagues.

One third of Dominican major league players are San Pedrans, who made their mark playing in the streets and leagues around the city. There are a number of major league training camps based in the region, the most notable of which is run by the San Francisco Giants.

Catching a game

If you happen to be in San Pedro between mid-November and February,

Left: Talking tactics
Opposite top: Going for the home run
Opposite: Baseball is an obsession in the Dominican Republic, whatever the players' level

you would be well advised to try and get some tickets to a Dominican professional-league game. Tickets sell out fast, especially if the match is between arch rivals, but you can usually get yourself a seat from a 'scalper' or 'tout'. The face-value of tickets is just a couple of US dollars. Expect to pay about five times that if you decide to go with an 'unofficial' seller.

The baseball stadium (Play de Beisbol) is located on the main road from Juan Dolio. It houses the local team, Las Estrellas Orientales. The colour of their uniform is green, along with the roof of the stadium and pretty much everything else around. If you want to blend in on the day, wear the local team colour.

Attending a baseball match in the Dominican is very different from the atmosphere of your typical American match. Spectators follow the 'more is more' theory of life, and the sound levels have to be heard to be believed. A few hours before the first ball is thrown is when the fun begins, as food-sellers, merengue musicians, touts and car park attendants stake their claim to a prime position and wait it out for the crowds to arrive – and arrive they do. Music, drumming, singing, cheering and jeering continue outside the stadium and inside it, and the noise is sustained before, during and after the game, no matter what the final score. Overwhelmingly colourful, this is spectator sport as art and adventure.

La Romana

Michael Jackson and Lisa Marie Presley put La Romana on the map when they chose this five-star resort community as the place to get married back in 1994, but it has been a favourite with the jet-set for much longer. Fashion designer and Dominican native Oscar de la Renta had a great deal of involvement in the resort's formative years, and especially with the town's premier property, Casa de Campo. His sheen has certainly rubbed off on the place, as it has become the destination of choice for moneyed visitors – and for good reason.

View of Casa de Campo, La Romana

History and geography

The town itself isn't really all that special. Situated beyond the rivers Soco and Cumayasa, La Romana is firmly focused around the massive Central de la Romana sugar mill, still the largest employer in the city. When the mill opened in 1917, it was the most technologically advanced of its day, but it's hard to imagine that when you look at the crumbling, rusting building of today.

The mill opened just as world sugar prices were soaring, sparking a demand for labour that brought families to the town from all over the country. Thanks to the mill, La Romana is still the largest sugar town in the Dominican – and the unofficial headquarters of the industry. Throughout the night you will be able to see and hear trains chugging through the town, loaded with sugar ready for export.

To give an idea of just how powerful the mill is, it currently employs over 20,000 people. La Romana's population sits at around 100,000 – that translates into 20 per cent of the town directly reliant on the success or failure of world sugar prices.

American investment has played a strong role in directing the fortunes of the town. In 1967, the mill was sold to the US conglomerate Gulf & Western, who invested heavily in the local economy and infrastructure. The company diversified into cattle and cement in order to reduce La Romana's reliance on all things sweet. They also developed and built the Casa de Campo resort in order to bring tourism to this corner of the country. A number of the town's schools, churches, parks and homes have been rebuilt, constructed from scratch or restored thanks to the generosity of the company.

Gulf & Western sold off their Dominican holdings to the Cuban-American Fanjul family in the mid-1980s. The family continued Gulf & Western's tradition of assisting the local community, and has helped transform the city into one of the most employed locales in the country. This fact continues to draw the rural poor in the hope of finding work. As a result, the city is one of the fastest-growing in the Dominican.

Parque Central

Like other Dominican towns, the central park is a popular congregation point. Small in size, it features a number of obelisks, and serves as a good place in which to ponder life as the buzz of industrial activity swarms around you.

There are a number of brightly coloured homes around the park, all of which belong to the wealthier executives who work for the sugar mill. Around the town centre, housing isn't quite so plush and should be avoided. La Romana's town hall and parish church are situated directly on the Parque Central and are worth a quick peek if you are inclined.

Things to do

If you're in town in winter, then a visit to the Michelin baseball stadium should be on the cards. While it doesn't offer the jaw-dropping sights of games in Santo Domingo or San Pedro de Macorís, it's still a great place to get in touch with Dominican culture. The

Poolside at Casa de Campo

home team is consistently ranked at the bottom of the Dominican league, so don't go expecting any baseball miracles. The stadium is located at the corner of Abreu and Luperón, in the west end of the city.

Immediately west of the arena is the Municipal Market. While most of the stalls concentrate on everyday household goods, meat and produce, there are still a few traders who specialise in *bótanica* items, suitable for use in your next voodoo ceremony. For arts and crafts, go instead to the Mercado Modelo, located one block north of the Parque Central at the corner of Ramón and Fay Juan de Utrera. While the selection isn't as good as in other towns, it's a nice place to browse through, especially if you are waiting for transport to other parts of the country – domestic buses depart from just outside its entrance.

Casa de Campo

Considered the finest resort in the Dominican, Casa de Campo is a pleasurable complex of 150 luxury private villas set on over 7,000 acres of land and situated directly on the sea. The property isn't located in La Romana – it's too massive for that – but it is only a short drive east of town along the Carretera 4.

Two golf courses, 14 swimming pools, 24-hour tennis, horseback riding stables, polo grounds, personal trainers and a full-service spa are but a few of the extras offered to guests who choose to stay at this premium property. Madonna, Henry Kissinger, Elizabeth Taylor, and of course Michael Jackson

and Lisa Marie Presley are just a few of the well-known people who have enjoyed staying here.

Security levels here are extremely tight, and plastic wristbands are worn by guests at all times in order to ensure absolute safety. Those without the magic band are politely kept away from the accommodation quarters and relaxation centres. The only areas considered open to the public are the golf courses and shopping centre. With so much on offer, most tourists who book a stay find themselves never leaving the grounds, but you're still advised to rent a car, even if you have no plans to leave.

Because the property is so big, getting around poses a few problems, especially for the elderly or those with mobility difficulties. There is a system of shuttle buses, but they are famously slow and infrequent. If there is one reason to stay here, however, it is for the hotel's private beach – the Playa Minitas. This is a stunning stretch of sand protected by a shallow coral reef. According to Dominican law, all beaches are open to the public, so you are technically in the right if you decide to try and sneak in. You should be fine as long as you don't ask for a towel.

A small island, 2km (a mile) offshore, called Isla Catalina, is also within shooting distance of Casa de Campo and is well worth a trip. The resort has numerous shuttle boats that make the outward and return journey throughout the day. The island itself offers a lovely shaded pavilion and restaurant for guests to enjoy.

About the only criticism that can be levelled at Casa de Campo is that its food quality falls firmly into the bland international buffet school of all-inclusive thought. If fine dining is what you are after, you may be out of luck.

Altos de Chavón

Perched on a cliff overlooking the Río Chavón is this high-end shopping centre. Inside are numerous boutiques designed to appeal to the high-end clientele who call Casa de Campo home. While the complex is located on the Casa de Campo grounds, it is open to all, and you don't need to be a guest to drop by. The design is very faux – think artificially aged limestone, fake cobblestones and kitsch exteriors; but there are a few finds hidden amongst the tourist tat. Amongst the better options are a museum housing a good collection of pre-Columbian artefacts, and a reliable designer jewellery shop, Everett Designs, which specialises in good-quality pieces of amber and larimar.

Welcome to La Romana

Parqué Nacional del Este

Sitting in the extreme southwest of the country is the expansive Parqué Nacional del Este, a large peninsula that includes the small island of Saona. This is the Dominican for true adventure lovers and wilderness fiends. There is a maze of trails on offer to take you through and near the forests, caves and cliffs that make up the 310sq km (120sq miles) of protected land. Birdlovers will especially enjoy spotting some of the 112 known species of birds, eight of which are endemic to the island.

The perfect wilderness: the path to adventure

Even with the huge number of trails available for exploration, a vast amount of the park is completely inaccessible. No roads lead directly into the interior, and the truly determined will need to hire boats from the nearby town of Bayahibe to penetrate some of the more glorious locations.

Look sharp

If you do decide to hike, be aware of both wasps and tarantulas, as there are tons of both, all determined to get in the way of you having an enjoyable time. Be prepared by wearing plenty of mosquito repellent, and do not approach the nasty spiders. They won't harm you unless you annoy them first.

As you trek through the woods, look out for the *Hispaniolan solenodon*, an endangered species. *Hispaniolan solenodons* are rather weedy-looking rodents with long snouts and small eyes. They are pretty difficult to spot unless you have keen eyesight. The other two endangered species that can be found in the area are a little more common. These are the West Indian manatee and bottleneck dolphins, and can be seen in the water travelling through the strait that separates Isla Saona from the mainland.

Aerial shot of Parqué Nacional del Este

Isla Saona

The most popular part of the park is Isla Saona, a small island situated off the southern coast. Once known as an untouched paradise, traffic here has increased to such a point that it is not the idyllic location that it once was – but it still has plenty of enough merit to warrant a visit. The beaches are like something out of Robinson Crusoe, with long stretches of coconut-tree-lined sand that seemingly go on for miles. Go beyond that and you will find near-empty mangrove swamps that have two small clusters of fishermen living within.

Boats to the island can be chartered in the nearby resort town of Bayahibe. Most will drop you off at Mano Juan, a tiny collection of brightly coloured shacks. These stand close to a 4km (2.5-mile) trail that will take you further inland, away from the bulk of the tourists. If possible, try and bring a packed lunch, as the only restaurant on Saona is very pricy and does not warrant the extra cost.

Birdlovers will discover many new species

If all you want is a place to dip your feet into the sea, wind your way to the Piscina Natural – a lovely little lagoon, perfect for keeping cool on a hot day. Better yet, go with an independent captain and ask him to take you away from the action. There are a number of other beaches along Saona's coast that see far fewer foreign tourists.

LA ALETA

Before the days of Columbus, the region around that now contains the Parqué Nacional del Este was home to a large Taino population. Deep in the wilds of the park, remnants of the society can be found in the form of a significant excavation site known as La Aleta.

La Aleta's population was murdered in what is perhaps one of the most gruesome episodes of Spanish colonial history. It began when a Taino chieftain was disembowelled by a Spanish attack dog. Incensed locals began to riot, and the Spanish responded by killing 7,000 of their people.

Tranquillity among the trees

Punta Cana

Punta Cana is a purpose-built beachside resort town constructed specifically for the tourist industry. Nothing much existed here before the dawn of the travelling age – and nothing much has developed since the first hotels were built in the early 1980s. The first tourist resort to hit town was Club Med in 1981. This was followed in 1988 by the Punta Cana Beach Resort.

Trees sway in the breeze at Punta Cana

It's easy to see why the location was developed with tourism in mind. The coast offers some spectacular beaches and excellent diving. A new international airport is bringing more and more tourists into the region every day, and further development is on the cards in the near future.

The town itself is drawing a number of the Dominican and Spanish elite to build holiday homes in the region. Both singer Julio Iglesias and designer Oscar de la Renta own property in the nearby, exclusive Los Corales complex.

Restful resorts

Punta Cana is the perfect place to stay if you are looking to enjoy your fun in the sun in a full-service resort and don't mind the fact that you won't experience any Dominican culture while doing so. Most of the beaches in the region are privately owned, even though according to Dominican law this practice is illegal. You won't get very far debating with the resort security if you do attempt to sneak onto what they consider to be private property, but it is possible to gain access if you look sufficiently moneyed and 'Western tourist' enough.

The resorts of Punta Cana host approximately 700,000 visitors every year. Despite this figure, the beaches remain surprisingly empty. It is possible to walk for more than 30km (19 miles) along the Punta Cana coastline, if you have the strength or inclination. If you travel in the off-season, you may even be able to do this without facing more than just a handful of travellers. Resort beaches tend to offer a range of services and amenities, namely deck chairs, umbrellas, food shacks and souvenir stands.

Because they are privately owned and maintained, you will experience far less hassle than you would on other public beaches on the island, specifically Boca Chica, Sosúa and Cabarete. Of course, what you gain in silence you will lose in local colour. You will not find too many merengue music dens or worker-focused bars in this town. Rather your merengue will be sung in English in the resort disco, and free lessons will be offered by the hotel staff. It's less colourful but a lot less chaotic – and you won't feel embarrassed if you get your steps wrong because everyone else will be in the same boat as you.

Stormy weather

Punta Cana's geographic location on the extreme east coast of the country translates into a balmy climate – for the majority of the year. However, don't be lulled into a false sense of security: in hurricane season, this region of the country gets the worst hit of all, and you would be well advised to check weather reports on a regular basis if you visit between May and November. Tropical Storm Jeanne battered the town in 2004 and a number of hotels are only just completing repairs.

Sail away

If you are planning to include the Dominican as part of a Caribbean sailing journey, Punta Cana offers an excellent marina, with capacity for 22 yachts, immigration and customs services. Sailing conditions are excellent, and a night watchman and permanent guard ensure that security is a priority. There are not usually any problems if you pull in with no advance notice; however, if you are arriving from international waters, it is a good idea to give them a 24-hour warning.

Dancing dolphins at an aquarium in Santo

Bávaro

Considered by many to be an extension of the Punta Cana strip is the area of Bávaro. Formerly a collection of fishing villages, the local community has now abandoned any claim it may have once had on the sea in favour of yet more resort hotels catering to the tourist trade. Look closely and you may still be able to spot a shack or two hidden amongst the concrete and glass.

The Bávaro Beach pool

Cabeza de Toro

At the easternmost point of the island is Cabeza de Toro; this is a government-supported project designed to help the local community by allowing locals to sell arts and crafts directly from their huts. If you are a fan of Haitian primitive art, be sure to keep an eye out for the Plaza Artisanal, where there are literally dozens of stalls selling the stuff. This is not necessarily of the highest quality, or the work of the most well-known artists, but it's pleasant enough to look at and will certainly cheer up a wall when you are back at home.

Naïve art on sale in tourist shops

Resort central

In the heart of the action are a grouping of three resorts set in the middle of protected mangroves and wetland: the Catalonia Bávaro, Allegro Resort Bávaro Grand and the Natura Park. These are the places to stay if you want to be a little closer to the trappings of the town, yet still want to enjoy the pristine beaches for which the area is known. Of the three, the Allegro is the most modern; it was completed in 2000. It is also the most convenient, as public buses stop directly outside its entrance.

Ironically, while the beaches are raved about, they are regularly improved with imported sand and cleaned by a massive team of maintenance workers every morning at dawn.

Go north

The north coast of Bávaro is the most resort-heavy section of the beach, with a number of luxury properties and a casino for visiting travellers. There is a good shopping market in this pocket of town. Known as Bibijagua, it's essentially a large, covered collection of stalls selling typical Dominican souvenirs. While most of the stuff offered for sale is fine, there are a few exceptions: the cigars are often fake, the Haitian art is mass-produced and there are turtles, shells and stuffed sharks on offer that if purchased and brought home could get you into serious trouble (they are protected by international treaties). If you were caught carrying such items, they would be impounded – and you would not get any money back for your troubles.

Cows grazing near Hato Mayor

A guard controls entry to cyclone-hit beaches

JUST SAY NO!

If you're staying anywhere in the Punta Cana/Bávaro region, then chances are you will see one of the numerous billboards enticing you to visit Manatí Park. If you have any love for wildlife, then don't go. This controversial tourist attraction boasts performing horses, dolphins, sea lions, turtles, birds and a talking parrot show.

The park originally opened in 1997 with four bottlenose dolphins caught in the wild and purchased from Cuba. Two more were grabbed from local waters. Since then, four of them have died. Instead of doing something to improve their conditions, the holding company that operates the park just keeps buying more dolphins to replace the ones that they lose. A number of marine biologists and organisations have appealed to the park to end the cruelty, to no avail.

If you do decide to go, please do not be tempted to pay the additional charge to swim with the dolphins. It is contact with humans that is killing the creatures, as their bacteria levels and finally their immune systems are affected. That, combined with the small size of their tanks, is a recipe for disaster.

Parqué Nacional los Haitises

The Parqué Nacional los Haitises is a 208sq km (80sq mile) park just west of Sabana de la Mar on the south coast of Samaná Bay. The park is known for its lush hills that reach toward the ocean in undulant waves of green. A boat is a necessity if you are looking to explore the region, as large sections of the land are inaccessible.

A boat is essential to explore the park

The bulk of the park is covered in mangrove swamp that protects a number of 'secret' Taino caves, plants, birds and marine life. Only a small portion of the park is actually open to the public, and organised tours are often the only way you can explore.

Wet, wet, wet

If you prefer to stay dry, then you may be in the wrong place. The park is the wettest spot in the country; it receives more rainfall than anywhere else in the Dominican. This encourages a wide range of subtropical plants to flourish that are not found in other parts of the island. Bamboo, ferns and bromeliads are just a few examples of the plant life that can be seen here.

Birds rule the roost

The coast is famous for holding the country's largest untouched expanse of red and white mangroves. If you do take a boat tour to the park, you'll have to manoeuvre your way through these seemingly impenetrable trees before you reach the dense rainforest.

Ruta Litoral

The standard boat trip to the park is known as the Ruta Litoral. This route takes you round most of the park's highlights and is the most commonly recommended trip for those wanting a day-trip. The first stop on this tour is the Cueva Arena, an amply sized grotto that features a range of Taino cave drawings depicting images of daily life, including families, hunting scenes, religious icons and local water creatures.

If you have an interest in pirate history, try and extend your stay at this point to include a bit of extra time in the Cayo Willy Simons, once the hideaway of the notorious pirate. Look out for the dozens of pelicans, herons, terns, frigates and falcons that nest close to the entrance.

The next stop is the grottos of San Gabriel and Remington. These caves feature Taino faces carved directly into the walls. Once again, these caves hosted a number of pirates in their time, including Jack Banister, John Rackham and the infamous Cofresí. On your way you will pass the remains of a 100-year-old banana wharf, notable only for the number of pelicans that nest on the rotting pilings.

The final stop on the journey is Cueva de la Linea, named because it was once intended as the location for a railroad station for transporting the sugar cane grown in abundance in the area. In fact, the station was never built, and today the sugar cane no longer exists either.

Before the days of Columbus, the cave was a Taino temple. Archaeologists have ascertained this through the discovery of a guardian face carved at the entrance, the residue of campfire smoke left over from religious ceremonies, and through the descriptive pictographs that line the interior walls.

Arranging a tour

A boat tour can be arranged in Sabana

The tangled roots of the mangrove swamps

de la Mar and will cost from around RD$800 for up to six people on the boat, RD$50 for the park fee and RD$300 for the services of a guide. Guides can be booked at the national park office at the town port in the east end of Sabana.

National park office, Sabana de la Mar. Tel: (809) 556 7333.

Negotiating densely thicketed waterways by boat

Samaná

Officially named Santa Bárbara de Samaná but known by everyone as Samaná, this small town of 40,000 is the capital of Samaná Province and the gateway to some of the country's most remote beaches and centres for wildlife watching. The area is known for rolling landscapes filled with coconut groves and prettily coloured houses, and is literally the 'end of the line' of the north coast's highway number four.

Spectacular view over Samaná Bay

History

Samaná was settled more recently than other towns; it can only trace its founding back to 1756, when a number of settlers from the Canary Islands arrived in the area at the invitation of the then-governor Rubio y Peñaranda.

The cultural mix grew more interesting at the beginning of the 19th century, when hundreds of freed American slaves ended up in the region and decided to establish roots here. As such, there are a number of Protestants in the community with decidedly English last names, such as Smith, King or Williams.

The port of Samaná

Prized possession

In 1795, the Spanish gave Napoleon Bonaparte control over the entirety of Hispaniola in exchange for territories in Spain that he controlled. Bonaparte dreamed of establishing a New World capital in Samaná, but he quickly saw his dreams dashed thanks to a Haitian revolution, two British invasions and dissent from his French commanders. It was almost a decade before Napoleon was finally able to take control of the region, but he could not enjoy his triumph for very long, as the Haitian revolutionaries and another British invasion soon forced him to give up his claims.

Fighting flames

It's a bit difficult to picture a Napoleonic metropolis sitting where Samaná currently stands. The city is decidedly modern, with few visible old landmarks thanks to a fire that swept through much of the city in 1946. The cathedral – always the focal point of any Dominican town – is new in design, the streets are broad and the restaurants and hotels are all purpose-built.

As the birthplace of the former President Balaguer, Samaná benefited (or suffered, depending on how you look at it) from strong government interest and investment throughout much of the 1970s. Determined to transform the town into the leading tourist destination on the island, Balaguer tore down any remaining old buildings in order to create a utopian resort on a grand scale.

A bridge was built to connect the city with two islands that lay a few hundred metres offshore, and a restaurant was constructed on the furthest island to cater to the masses that Balaguer assumed would soon be flocking to the region. Unfortunately, his defeat in the 1978 elections meant that the plans had to be scrapped, and the investment and infrastructure went to Playa Dorada instead.

HARVEST FESTIVALS

Samaná's African-American community is famous for its annual series of harvest festivals, held every Friday from late August to the end of October. The festivals are large community feasts that include church music, folk tales and storytelling. This tradition is closely related to the Yarn Celebrations and Rice Festivals of West Africa.

There are a number of small churches that serve the English-speaking African community, which is scattered throughout the surrounding countryside. Each week the celebration is held in a different church. If you are interested in attending, check the bulletin board at the back of La Churcha (see p87) for dates and locations. The final festival of the series is always held in La Churcha at the end of October.

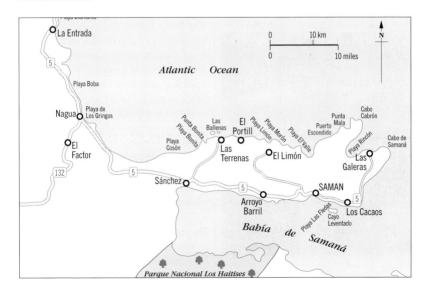

Walk: Sultry Samaná

The city is a little short on specific sights of interest, but if you find charming neighbourhoods, winding streets and a sense of community appealing, then you will enjoy a walk round this beautiful place.

Allow: 3 hours

Begin your stroll at the Malecón.

1 The Malecón

Sprinkled with outdoor cafés, simple shopfronts and small but perfectly formed parks, the Malecón functions as Samaná's body, mind and spirit. In high season, the nights are electric with atmosphere, as the restaurants and bars spill out into the evening air.

Walk towards the port at the centre of the strip.

2 Samaná port

Elevated balconies in Samaná port

City life

provide excellent vantage points from which to examine the hustle and bustle of the city and the harbour. As the departure point for trips to Cayo Levantado, Sabana de la Mar, the Parqué Nacional los Haitises, and for the numerous humpback whale-watching boats that cruise the bay in winter, the port is always busy.

Proceed to the harbour's western promontory until you see a rickety bridge.

3 The bridge to nowhere

The bridge to nowhere links Samaná to the islands of Cayo Linares and Cayo Vigia – and is hardly ever used. You can access the bridge by going through an unlocked gate in the car park behind the Cayacoa Resort. Don't be put off by the graffiti-covered ruins that lead up to the structure; the views of the bay and the town are stunning. For a ghostly feeling, go to the end of the bridge and climb up a muddy slope to examine the ruins of a restaurant that was originally scheduled to open on Cayo Vigia, but never did.

This whole section of town, while beautiful in its seclusion, also serves to remind citizens of what might have been, had Balaguer managed to make good on his promise to transform

Samaná with tourist dollars.
Continue west past the Cayacoa Resort until you reach the beach.

4 Playa Escondido
The public beach is surprisingly underused. While there are many better-looking beaches a short distance from the town centre, if you don't have access to a car, this beach will do the trick.
Retrace your steps to the Malecón until you reach the bandstand. Take the next left and follow the street for about two blocks until you see a church on your right. The walk from the Cayo Vigia to the church is about 1.5km (1 mile), so take your time and stop if you need to.

5 La Churcha
This prefabricated, tin-roofed church was shipped over by the English

The bandstand on the Malecón

Methodist Church in 1823 and serves as the spiritual centre for the town's African-American residents, many of whom can trace their lineage back to freed American slaves. Today, it is known as the Dominican Evangelical Church and works closely with the African Methodist Episcopalian Church located a few blocks away.
La Churcha, Corner of Santa Bárbara and Duarte. Open: daily 9am–6pm.

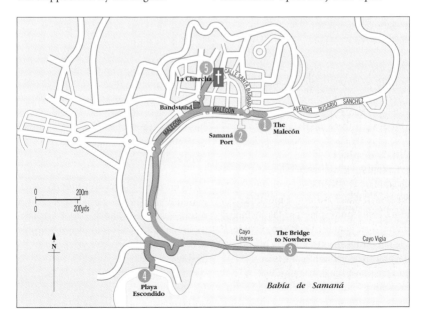

Whale-watching

If ever there was a sight to behold in the Dominican Republic, then it would have to be watching the humpback whales swimming in Samaná Bay. The spectacle begins every December, when the whales return to the region following nine months in the North Atlantic. The migration has occurred for as long as can be remembered. In caves surrounding the area, Taino art depicts the presence of whales, and Columbus made mention of the whales in writings dated 1493.

Whale-watching tours are a popular excursion

When to go
The best time to see the whales is between mid-January and mid-March, when the mammals are at their most active. It is during this period that you will spot courting rituals, as well as mothers teaching their calves basic survival skills. Mating and birthing also takes place in Samaná. The gestation period of the humpback whale is one year, so calves conceived here are also born here exactly twelve months later. There is a very good possibility that you'll see babies frolicking in the water as they learn how to stay alive.

Whale displays
Whales have a fascinating physical vocabulary that will keep you engrossed for hours. Watch out for some of the more common displays, which include: diving – arching the back and sticking the tail in the air immediately prior to a deep descent; lobtailing – a raise and smack of the tail against water; breaching – hurling the body above the surface of the water before landing with a great smack; chin breaching – raising the chin above the water surface to smack it against the water; and trumpet blows – a low blast that carries across several kilometres.

Whale song
The famed songs of the humpback whale are in reality a series of chirps and moans used as a form of communication. Only males use whale song, and it is heard much more frequently in Samaná than anywhere else in the world. This has led marine biologists to speculate that song is used as part of the mating ritual, since this is where the whales mate.

Whale-watching as an industry
As a draw for tourists, whale-watching is a relatively recent phenomenon, begun as late as the 1970s by an out-of-work scuba instructor by the name of Kim Beddall. Beddall has spent the last quarter-century protecting the whales by lobbying the government for funds and support.

More than 40 boats now offer whale-watching tours, all under the strict, eco-friendly restrictions set down by Beddall. Vessels must move slowly through the waters to avoid potential collisions, must always leave the waters in the same state in which they find them, and must remain a minimum distance away from the whales so that they don't feel threatened or harassed in any way.

Booking a whale tour

The best of the whale-watching trips can be had with the company that started it all – Kim Beddall's Whale Samaná/Victoria Marine company. The company charges a little more than most, with day-trips starting from US$38. If you want whale-watching to be the entire focus of your holiday, you can take part in week-long expeditions, which will give you more time to get 'up-close-and-personal' with the ocean's beautiful creatures. Week-long trips will take you a little further offshore – to the less frequently visited, yet just as fascinating, Silver Banks Sanctuary, which lies just north of the Samaná peninsula.

Acquatic Adventures are based out of Florida and offer a range of itineraries. *Acquatic Adventures. Tel: (305) 021 0211. Kim Beddall's Whale Samaná/Victoria Marine company, Malecón. Tel: (809) 538 2494.*

The fabulous display of the humpback whale

The Island's Top Five Beaches

With so many beaches to choose from, it is hard to know which ones to focus on. A pleasant beach can make the difference between a good holiday and a great one. Whether your idea of a fantastic beach is secluded and untouched or buzzing with activities, this list of the Dominican's top five spots will give you a great range of choice. Relaxation starts now…

Best for privacy – Playa Rincón

Playa Rincón is one of the most beautiful beaches in the Caribbean, thanks to its untouched sand, turquoise waters and lush coconut forest. Access to Playa Rincón is extremely difficult, making the journey here almost as fun and exciting as the final destination. Hidden from the rest of the Samaná peninsula by a jut of land at its eastern end, the beach is reached by taking a rocky road from Las Galeras. Dominican families love camping on the playa, drawn by warm, mostly placid waters. Definitely the place to go for that romantic stroll you've always dreamed of.

Best for views – Playa Runcia

Dominican mountains plunge down to bleached sand in what is probably one of the north shore's most beautiful beaches. Enjoy a spot of local rum while you savour the mountain views hovering in the near distance. The inhabitants of local shacks provide a touch of live music to add atmosphere to the proceedings. Reach this perfect playa on the road west from El Castillo, near La Isabela, around the lagoon.

Best for activities – Cabarete

Cabarete is considered one of the finest windsurfing locales in the world, but the fun doesn't stop there. Kite-surfing, scuba diving, snorkelling, mountain biking and one of the best nightlife scenes in the country are also on offer to the excitable international crowds. Adding to the fun is one of the Dominican's finest adventure tour operators – Iguana Mama. If you like your holiday to be packed with thrills, you should definitely find time for a trip here on your itinerary.

Best for snorkelling and diving – La Isabela

La Isabela, on the Dominican's north coast, may be better known as the place where Christopher Columbus decided to establish a settlement, but it also boasts an incredible array of underwater life, thanks to a large and relatively healthy coral reef located just offshore. While snorkelling supplies aren't exactly ample (bring your own equipment if you want to make the most out of the experience), the colours on offer will blow your mind. If you made the mistake of deciding not to include this slice of Columbus's past on your holiday, the snorkelling options should be more than enough to change your mind.

Best for people-watching – Santo Domingo's Malecón

In the Dominican Republic, a town's Malecón is always the hub of activity. Nowhere is this more evident than in the capital, Santo Domingo, where the Malecón is the centre of business life, the focal point for romance, a hotbed of five-star international hotels and the crown-holder of café culture. A typical

day will see dancers practising merengue moves on the sidewalk, American businessmen closing their latest Caribbean deal, and teenagers discovering true love amongst the waves.

Immerse yourself in it all by pulling up a chair at any of the cafés that line the route. If you have the money, you could also try checking into one of the pricy hotels along the strip and requesting a beachside view. You will not regret it.

Opposite top: Peace and quiet at Playa Rincón
Opposite below: Palm trees fringe the beach at Las Teresas
Top: Beached boats at Punta Rucia
Above: Children head for the waves
Left: The tranquil waters of Playa Ensenata

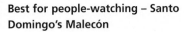

Cabarete

Just 20 years ago, the town of Cabarete had just two hotels – and neither of them were much to write home about. Today, that figure has changed drastically. Of all the towns along the north coast, this is probably the one with the most action – particularly if you're a building developer. Cabarete's popularity can be traced back to 1984, when the renowned professional windsurfer Jean Laporte stumbled upon the town and discovered what he thought were near-perfect conditions in which to practise his beloved sport (*see pp96–7*).

Pull up a chair and relax on Cabarete beach

Laporte's discovery attracted fellow lovers of water sports, who in turn drew the interest of hotel chains and adventure sports companies. Over time, the Dominican's ever-growing list of all-inclusive resort developers were also drawn to Cabarete, and the suburbs of the town are now littered with properties catering to the more-for-your-money masses.

Almost all of the town lies along the Carretera 5 and caters to tourists. Businesses line the two-lane highway for approximately 1km (half a mile). Where once there may have been locally owned and operated shops and services, there is now a plethora of places catering to the holiday crowd – mini-marts with micro-food, Internet cafés, cheap T-shirt shacks and the like.

Day and night
While the beach is pleasant enough, what mainly draws the muscled youth to this area is its reputation as a prime spot for windsurfing. Descending on this

corner of the world at all times of the year, keen water-sports aficionados go in search of perfect wind and waves.

Nightlife in Cabarete reflects the youthful nature of its visitors, and is much livelier and more varied than that of other towns in the region. Most nights will see bars stay open until the wee hours of the morning, playing a mix of Latin hits and Western sounds for an appreciative audience.

Getting your bearings
Surprisingly for a town with such high visitor numbers, Cabarete doesn't have a Ministry of Tourism office. However, the town's legendary sporting status has drawn numerous long-term residents from all corners of the globe. English, French, German and Spanish can be heard on street corners throughout Cabarete, so you are sure to find someone who can point you in the right direction.

For money exchange, the best bet is the bureau de change, which is located

The main street at Cabarete

Basking in the sun

access. One of the best options is La Mulata on the beach in the centre of town, where nine terminals offer Internet services from 9am–1am every day of the week. The burgers are not too bad either. Another good option is the News Café. Six terminals are set up in a refreshing, air-conditioned café, serving up light bites, salads and fresh juices. The café is open from 8am–10pm daily.

Keeping healthy

One of the north shore's finest medical centres is located in Cabarete; it has probably developed to cope with the number of windsurf-related injuries suffered by unwary international visitors. If you need some medical attention for any reason, then head over to the Servi-Med Medical Office on the west side of town. Services are available 24 hours a day. Both English and Spanish-speaking physicians are on call. *Servi-Med Medical Office. No formal address. Tel: (809) 571 0964.*

Feasts and festivities

February is 'happiness' month in Cabarete and celebrations permeate this period. Special events hosted by local businesses are held every weekend, varying in experience from live music to sport races. The fourth weekend is traditionally the busiest, as the town rolls out the red carpet to professional windsurfers for the Dominican national surfing and windsurfing competition.

June is another month of windsurf-themed partying as the third week of the month brings the Encuentro Classic – a series of courses for windsurfers at all levels of experience from feeble to first-

immediately opposite the Sun & Surf Hotel. The exchange rate here is much more competitive than at other places in town. Canadian and US dollars are accepted, in addition to euros.

Postal services are non-existent in Cabarete, so if you need to send something, you will either have to make a trip to nearby Sosúa, or use a private company called Domex. Domex has mailboxes in all the major hotel and gift shops in town. Unfortunately, its service is just as poor as the regular Dominican government-operated post.

Keeping in touch

Even though there are no post offices in town, there are still ways in which you can keep in touch with the outside world. Due to the large number of international resident and long-term visitors, e-mail and Internet access is good. A large number of the shops along the Carretera 5 offer what is laughingly referred to as 'high-speed' Internet

class. The town turns into one gigantic disco and drinking den during the festivities, becoming the party capital of the Dominican Republic.

Outside of town

Go south of Cabarete to visit El Choco National Park, a green spot known for its wide array of birdlife. However, be very careful if you decide to undertake explorations of the area. The trails are largely underdeveloped and the dense brush makes navigation extremely difficult.

Also located in the park are the Caves of Cabarete. Sounding a lot more interesting than they actually are, the caves are really just a set of holes that have been illuminated with electric light. Fenced off from the public, there is actually little to warrant you going out of your way to see.

The entrance to the park is located down a turnoff west of town. Organised tours are available if required, and are run on Mondays to Fridays from 9am–5pm. The down-side is that they are pretty expensive. The highlight of the tour is a swim in an underground pool.

Playa Encuentra is another day-trip option located 4km (2.5 miles) west of Cabarete on the Carretera 5. This is where the professional windsurfers come, drawn by some of the best waves in the Caribbean. Between 6am and 8am are the best times to see the pros at work, as 6m (20ft) waves come crashing towards the beach. In order to fully enjoy the truly amazing tricks on view, bring a pair of binoculars, as most of the action lies a few metres offshore.

ADVENTURE AND EXCITEMENT

Cabarete is an excellent place from which to organise adventure tours to the interior, and the best way to do this is through an incredible company known as Iguana Mama. Mountain-bike tours are the bread and butter of this eco-friendly tour operator, but its hiking trips to Pico Duarte also come highly recommended. When it comes to quality, the company cannot be beaten. All of its products are top-of-the-line, and guides almost always speak fluent English.

Other tours available to interested holidaymakers include whale-watching cruises, catamaran sailing, deep-sea fishing, kayaking (both river and open-water) and horseback riding. If you've got the time and are looking to see more than just the bar and the beach, then Iguana Mama should be your first stop.

Iguana Mama, East end of town. Tel: (809) 571 0008. www.iguanamama.com

Are you ready for the adventure?

W i n d s u r f ' s   U p

If ever there was a town that was built for windsurfing, then it's Cabarete. Conditions here are considered so perfect by those in the know that it is a marvel that there's any room left in the water for anyone without a board under their feet and a sail to guide them.

Cool conditions

So what makes it so amazing? Well, the first element is the winds. The trade winds in this region normally blow from the east. This means that they cut across the bay from right to left, allowing easy access to both the offshore reefs and back to the beach when you decide to undertake the return journey.

Professional windsurfers also appreciate the surf generated by the offshore reef. For expert wave riders, the foamy sea makes spectacular jumps and

tricks possible. But, the reef also helps in other ways, by preventing rough seas from entering the bay. This keeps the water inland mostly calm on all but the stormiest of days.

For beginners, the morning is the perfect time to try the sport: the normally gentle breezes combined with flat water make conditions ideal for attempting to get upright. This is especially true in the summer when the sea is at its calmest.

Kite-surfing

Sister-sport to windsurfing, kite-surfing is what rules the waves just 2km (a mile) west of Cabarete near Punta Goleta. Cabarete is very much on the cutting edge of this new experience, and you will find numerous outfitters there, eager to help visitors try it for themselves.

Kite-surfing uses a huge kite, rather than a sail, for power. Less wind is required, meaning that most enthusiasts can get up and running on days when windsurfers are left drinking coffee at the beachside café.

Kitting up

The best windsurf and kite-surf outfitters are right on the beach. Pricing does not actually vary too much (even though the posted rates may seem to differ on first glance), but the key to success is the make of equipment. Examine what's offered to you before you complete any transaction. And to make your life easier, try and choose a place that offers English-speaking staff, a wide selection of in-stock gear and a launch position on the beach – vital if the wind is playing up.

If you've brought your gear and find yourself in need of a repair, the best place in town to get things fixed is Cabarete Sail and Board Repair, located next to the Banana Boat hotel. There is no phone or schedule of appointments, so just take your gear along and hope they can fit you in.

School's in

If you are looking to learn either of the two exciting sister-sports, then Cabarete has a number of schools that will get you started. The key things to look out for when selecting any windsurf or kite-surf academy are: safety, English-language skills and quality of gear. This is not an occasion where it pays to go cheap. Some of the better schools are listed below.

Windsurf schools

Carib Bic Center. Tel: (809) 571 0649.
www.caribwind.com
Club Mistral. Tel: (809) 571 0770.
www.club-mistral.com
Fanatic. Tel: (809) 571 0861.
www.fanatic-cabarete.com
Vela/Spinout. Tel: (809) 571 0805.
www.velacabarete.com

Kitesurf schools

Cabarete Kitesurf. Tel: (809) 857 0148.
www.cabarete-kitesport.com
Dare2fly. Tel: (809) 571 0805.
www.dare2fly.com
Kite Excite. Tel: (809) 838 1225.
w.kiteexcite.com

Opposite top: First lesson
Opposite below: Windsurfs for hire
Above: An expert rides the waves
Below: The thrills of kite-surfing

Sosúa

Once the Dominican banana capital, the large resort town of Sosúa is now one of the north coast's most popular vacation destinations. From the mid-19th century until 1916, the town acted as the headquarters for the United Fruit Company, who used it as the port for their banana plantations. When the company left, so Sosúa's fortunes declined.

Another glorious beach: Playa Sosúa

Religious renaissance

It was not until the early 1940s that the town's fortunes began to improve. Transplanted European Jews, fleeing persecution from Nazi Germany, settled in the region – in fact, the Dominican Republic was one of the few countries in the Western hemisphere to permit Jews to immigrate. The result of this offer of hospitality was a mini-enclave of 350 Jewish families, mostly from Germany and Austria. These European settlers founded a network of slaughterhouses and dairies to produce cheese and sausages; these eventually brought prosperity to the region.

Prosperity to persecution

The success of the Jewish settlement brought resentment from Dominican locals, who envied and resented the Jewish presence, and the outlay of financial capital on what was perceived to be 'their' land. In the 1960s virtually the entire Jewish population was driven out as Dominican peasants moved on to the land used by the dairy farmers to graze their cows, cutting down most of the valuable timber on the surrounding hillsides to construct squatter communities. When it became obvious that local police would refuse to back them against these anti-Semitic acts, the Jewish community largely moved to the safer locales of Israel and the United States.

You can explore more of Sosúa's fascinating Jewish past with a visit to the Museum de la Comunidad Judía de Sosúa, located directly next to the local synagogue. Be sure to check ahead to ensure that the museum is open, as it is only accessible to the public at irregular times.

Museo de la Comunidad Judía de Sosúa, Calle Dr Alejo Martínez, near Calle Dr Rosen. Free.

Sleepy and sedate

In terms of physical sights, there is not that much in Sosúa – other than its world-class beach. As the resort town is better-established than others along the north coast, it tends to draw a sedate, older crowd who have been experiencing the town's charms for years, if not generations. Nightlife is limited to sipping a cold beer at a quiet beachside bar, or exploring the main street's bars and more vibrant trappings.

Orientation

Sosúa's main street into town is the Calle Duarte, which is also the main street off the highway (Carretera Gregorio Luperón). For the bulk of the town's bar, restaurant and shopping options, Calle Pedro Clisante is the place to come. The heart of Sosúa is therefore formed by the intersection of these two major streets. The beach is located only a short walk away.

Don't worry if your hotel is situated far from this lively district, since many hotels in town provide convenient shuttle services to take you from the property to the centre of town.

Motoconchos and taxis also regularly tout for business along these two major arteries, so you should not have any problem getting around.

El Batey

The district of El Batey, specifically around Calle Pedro Clisante, is either tourist hell or heaven, depending upon your point of view. Here you will be able to find everything, from hand-crafted shell nightlights to a string of plastic beads masquerading as amber.

If you need a quick and cheap bite, are looking to arrange onward transport or need a place to get your bearings,

A snorkeller's paradise: equipment ready for hire

then this is the place to head for. A large number of German immigrants call this corner home, which explains why you will be able to tuck into some surprisingly good schnitzel here.

Plying the Playa

The main reason for Sosúa's popularity is the beach – and justifiably so. Shaped like a crescent and surrounded by cliffs, this 250m (820ft) long stretch of sand is probably one of the most geographically blessed in the Dominican. The horseshoe-shaped bay means that the waters are largely calm, and the undertow isn't as strong as at other playas in the region.

Scuba divers are attracted by tranquil waters

Snorkellers and scuba divers especially love coming to the bay due to the placid nature of the water – Sosúa's waters are calm for 95 per cent of the year. Look for stalls that sell equipment; they are located just behind the sand, in amongst the busy row of seafood restaurants, souvenir shops and mom-and-pop trinket salespeople. The quality of the equipment might be variable, but their masks and fins should do the trick if you are looking to explore the reef located just outside the inlet.

Los Charamicos

The barrio of Los Charamicos is situated on the western edge of the playa. This is definitely the 'real people' part of town, which caters to the local populace. Here is where you will find narrow streets, hanging laundry, merengue music and barefoot children playing on the asphalt.

There are a number of recommended open-air eateries on the district's main square, Calle Arzeno. The views of the beach are absolutely splendid, and in addition you tend to get a more 'authentic' meal.

The truly adventurous can keep going further west, to the far edge of town, where the local cockfighting arena lies on Calle Morris. Tuesdays and Saturdays are the days to mark in your calendar if you want to witness this bloody, cruel and yet incredibly 'Dominican' sporting event (from 3–7pm). Try the Club Gallístico Los Charamicos. Tickets for gallery standing room are cheaper than for the seats at ground-floor level. However, be warned: the crowd tends to get quite enthusiastic.

Museo de la Comunidad Judía (Jewish Museum) at Sosúa

Playa Chiquita

If you find yourself invited to visit Playa Chiquita, then you might want to think twice about it. From an anthropological point of view, this beach is fascinating – considered by locals to be the best beach in the area. But here is where the interest ends. The sand is rubbish-strewn and not particularly inviting, and the noise of screaming children and rambunctious teenagers can reach ear-splitting levels. The only day when the playa should be on your must-see list is on 13 June, when the beach plays host to Sosúa's *fiesta patronal* in honour of San Antonio.

PROSTITUTION

During the 1980s and early 1990s, Sosúa developed a bit of a reputation for the number of Haitian and Dominican prostitutes who chose to come here to ply their trade. The AIDS epidemic did much to bring this industry crashing down, as the island of Hispaniola registered among the highest numbers of patients living with the disease in the world. Today, the relics of this tarnished past remain: single men exploring the streets of town alone are sure to get accosted by prostitutes and bar girls looking to make a buck and/or bring in potential clients.

Walk: The Playa Dorada Complex

If you're staying in Playa Dorada, then your main exercise may well be the walk from your poolside deckchair to the all-you-can-eat buffet. But, if you want to see just what attracts thousands of holidaymakers to the Playa Dorada complex (or just want to check out the facilities and layouts of the other hotel properties), then this walk is for you.

Allow: up to 6 hours, depending on how long you stop at each hotel and shopping complex along the way.

There are two main gates to the Playa Dorada complex. Begin this walk from the west gate on Route 5, walking away from the Carretera. At the first junction, turn right to get to your first stop – Puerto Plata Village.

1 Puerto Plata Village
A value-for-money, all-inclusive property with 380 rooms. Accommodation is cottage-style, designed to resemble the Victorian gingerbread architecture of Puerto Plata.

Guarding the gate at Playa Dorada Plaza

There is no direct beach access, but it is conveniently located for the golf course. *Walk back towards the main Playa Dorada road from the main entrance and cross into Jack Tar.*

2 Jack Tar Village, Puerto Plata Beach Resort and Casino
Built for the active traveller, Jack Tar caters to couples and singles looking for lots of 'stuff' to do. Jack Tar is one of the older properties in the complex, but all of the hotel rooms are nicely maintained. Definitely the stop of choice if jetskiing, parasailing and gambling are on your 'must-do' list.
Return to the main Playa Dorada road and continue walking away from the main gate. Rumba Heavens will appear on your left.

3 Rumba Heavens
Rumba Heavens is a budget three-star resort with only 192 rooms and suites. Rooms offer all the basics, but you shouldn't expect many frills. Most Playa Dorada guests visit the property for its

well-known disco.
Continue along the main road for a short distance and turn left. The driveway entrance to Playa Naco will be on your left.

4 Playa Naco Golf and Tennis

One for the kids: the Playa Naco is a 418-room, three-storey complex that boasts a games room, disco, kids activity centre, sauna, shops, doctor and on-site pharmacy. Close to the beach, the Playa Naco is great for water-lovers.
Go back down the driveway. Hotetur Dorado Club will be directly in front of you.

5 Hotetur Dorado Club

Another child-friendly resort, the Hotetur Dorado Club is one of the smallest; it also offers the least activity possibilities in the complex. There are only 165 rooms on site and the rooms tend to be on the small side. In the case of Hotetur Dorado, the all-inclusive tag is slightly misleading, as only local drinks are served free of charge.
Go back towards Rumba Heavens by turning left out of the driveway. Go left again once you reach the main Playa Dorada road. The Playa Dorado Plaza will be on your left.

6 Playa Dorada Plaza

A recent addition to the complex, the Playa Dorada Plaza is the first shopping mall on the north coast of the country. While the prices are high, it is pretty much true that 'you get what you pay for', as the quality of the wares is better than your average souvenir shop. Specialities include locally crafted

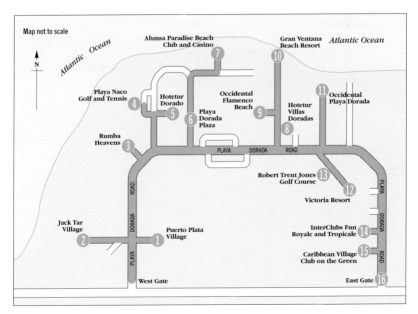

Wish you were here?: Playa Dorada offers some spectacular beaches

jewellery, ceramics and clothing. Dominican favourites such as cigars, larimar, amber, coffee and rum can all be purchased here, albeit at a slightly inflated price.

Turn left towards the beach away from the main Playa Dorada road and carry on until you reach the Ahmsa Paradise Beach Club and Casino.

7 Ahmsa Paradise Beach Club and Casino

One of the better options, the Ahmsa Paradise is located right on the beach, offers plenty of daily activities and has three restaurants with a wide selection of food that is better than your average buffet fare. Only local drinks are free of charge – but that's about the only downside to this resort.

Return to the main Playa Dorada road and continue away from the west gate. You will see the Hotetur Villas Doradas Beach Resort on your left.

8 Hotetur Villas Doradas Beach Resort

Standard three-star property surrounded on all sides by the resort road complex, making beach access a little annoying. The property's claim to fame is the variety of restaurants on-site, including a Chinese eatery.

Continue on the road away from the main Playa Dorada strip. The Occidental Flamenco Beach is on the left.

9 Occidental Flamenco Beach

The Occidental Flamenco Beach battles it out with the Gran Ventana (your next stop on the itinerary) for the hearts and wallets of moneyed five-star patrons.

Regular rooms are comfortable, but it's the suites in the Club Miguel Angel that should encourage you to start saving now. Each of the suites comes complete with private concierge and secretarial facilities, allowing you to combine business with lots of pleasure.

The actual complex is massive, with more than 582 rooms. There are plenty of bars, restaurants, discos, activities and a range of other facilities to choose from. The kids' club is highly recommended.

Continue along the same road away from the main Playa Dorada road. The Gran Ventana Beach Resort will be on your left.

10 Gran Ventana Beach Resort

The Gran Ventana is the newest property in the Playa Dorada complex. Located directly on the beach, this five-star resort caters to all tastes – from honeymooning couples looking for seclusion, to large families in need of activities galore to keep the kids occupied. Surprisingly for a resort of this quality, sporting activities are limited to one hour per day.

If you're up for a bit of adventure and don't mind a few patches of difficult terrain, walk away from the main west gate and along the coast until you reach the Occidental Playa Dorada (on your

A resort for all ages

right). Otherwise, return to the main Playa Dorada road and continue away from the main west gate. The Occidental Playa Dorada will be on your left.

11 Occidental Playa Dorada

A large pool area, casino and sports animation team keep patrons coming back to this 500-room, three-to-four star property. Perfect for those who want lots to do but don't have endless supplies of money.

Continue along the Playa Dorada road and take the next right turn. The Victoria Resort will be on your right.

12 Victoria Resort

If the idea of an all-inclusive holiday is not that appealing, but you like the idea of staying in the Playa Dorada complex because of its proximity to a range of activities, tourist-based nightlife and sandy beaches, then the Victoria Resort might be just the ticket. As one of the smaller resorts in Playa Dorada with only 190 rooms, the Victoria is also one of the friendliest. While it doesn't boast direct beach access or activities galore, it is the best choice for golfers, situated as it is right next to the course. Sports facility usage is restricted to one hour per day, but the property has beautiful mountain views and guests can eat à la carte every night if they desire.

Your next stop is located next to the main entrance of the Victoria Resort.

13 Robert Trent Jones Golf Course

Golf is one of the main draws to Playa Dorada, specifically in the form of this Robert Trent Jones-designed 18-hole course. Situated in the middle of the

complex, four of the holes are set beside the sea; there is also inland water to add interest and difficulty.

If you are staying at one of the hotels in Playa Dorada, green fees with caddy cost US$33. Tourists from outside the complex will pay approximately 10 per cent more. Some of the all-inclusive properties do offer deals on golfing, so if that is your sporting passion, it is worth researching whether your property is one of them.

Return to the Victoria Resort. The InterClubs Fun Royale & Tropicale is located due south of the property.

14 InterClubs Fun Royale and Tropicale

Another good property for golfers, the InterClubs is more your standard all-inclusive, offering 352 rooms in two- or three-storey buildings. Five restaurants are located on-site, including two that offer Brazilian and Spanish fare. A gym, sauna and kids' club also come as part of the package.

Continue along the main road towards the east gate. At the next junction, turn right. The Caribbean Village Club on the Green will be on the left.

15 Caribbean Village Club on the Green

The Caribbean Village Club on the Green offers a few options not found in any of the other resorts in the complex – it is specifically tailored to those who want to learn a little more about Dominican culture. In addition to the usual all-inclusive options, the property has a health club and spa, a special cigar-lovers' package that includes visits to local tobacco manufacturers, tastings, and an optional plantation tour. While the property doesn't have beachfront access, there are regular transports to the beach.

Continue walking to the east gate.

16 The east gate

The east gate is your best departure point if you are looking to get a taxi or *motoconcho* away from the complex to points further along the north coast. If you are on a budget, you can catch one of the numerous buses that pass by the gate. Both the east and west gates are also great places to pick up cheap gifts and crafts: there are plenty of stalls and sellers offering trinkets and souvenirs at both locations.

PLAYING THE CASINOS

Playa Dorada has three casinos in which to gamble your wages – Jack Tar Village, Ahmsa Paradise Beach Club and Occidental Playa Dorada Hotel. The casinos all feature both gaming tables and slot machines; the gaming tables can be played with either Dominican pesos or American dollars, but the slots only accept US dollars.

Do not change your money at the exchange counters in the casinos: the rates are probably the worst on the island.

Take a stroll along the palm-fringed beach

Puerto Plata

If you're coming to the Dominican Republic on holiday, then chances are that Puerto Plata will be the first (and possibly only) stop on your itinerary. The main city on the northern coast of the country, Puerto Plata is also a busy seaport, and boasts one of the largest airports in the country. It is a shame that the town itself is rarely visited by tourists.

Cruise ships berth in the busy seaport

Geography lessons

The town itself is the third largest in the Dominican Republic, situated between Mt Isabel de Torres and the sea. One of the most popular excursions is a cable-car ride to the top of the mountain – an elevation of 779m (2,556ft).

Sweeping along the seafront is the Malecón, a 5km (3-mile) stretch of road that sweeps from the San Felipe fortress to Long Beach. Like much of the city, however, this road has seen better days, and takes drivers past clusters of shantytowns and garbage-strewn streets. The old city is very compact and easy to explore (*see walk p110*) offering numerous points of interest, specifically from the city's booming 19th-century past.

History lessons

Founded in 1502, Puerto Plata – 'Silver Port' – was named by Christopher Columbus, who saw the water glistening silver in the sun as he sailed past the bay. For many years, the town acted as a supply stop for merchant ships sailing between the Caribbean and the Old World. Unfortunately, its geography made it prone to pirate attacks.

Crackdowns on the local populace by the Spanish government drove many away from the north coast during the 17th century. It wasn't until 1751 that the port started to build at a rapid rate as Canary Islanders moved into the area with the assistance of the Spanish crown.

The 19th and early 20th centuries brought prosperity to the region, as tobacco from the Cibao region became prized by European consumers. Many merchants (mostly of German descent) moved in; their wealth resulted in the construction of a plethora of luxury mansions in what is now the old town.

The Great Depression signalled the end of Puerto Plata's brief success. It was not until the 1960s and the dawn of the tourism age that financial hope returned to the local populace as resorts sprang up and international travellers arrived in the region. Today, it is known more for its all-inclusive resorts and sun-drenched beaches than for its cigars and sugar cane.

What to see

The main sight in town and one of the first you will see if you arrive by cruise ship is the colonial fortress, the Fortaleza de San Felipe. The oldest fortress in the New World, the Fortaleza sits on a promontory at the west side of town. Constructed to provide protection against the constant pirate attacks that plagued the city during much of the 17th century, the fortress has since been used as a prison and a museum. Today, the structure contains some rusty examples of armoury, cannons and swords from the period. Weather and salt-water is rapidly eating through the bricks, so if you want to enjoy the view from the turrets, do so before it is too late. The lighthouse is also slowly disintegrating, and is now considered an endangered structure. Built in 1879, the cast-iron lighthouse was last repaired in 1979. Today, only the shell remains, as the sea air has destroyed the spiral staircase and seriously corroded the bulk of what remains.

Guided tours are available but not recommended as the structure is in such a state of disrepair. Admission fee.

A cable car ride to the summit of Pico Isabel de Torres

Walk:
Victorian Puerto Plata

Back in the 19th century, the city of Puerto Plata was a goldmine for European tobacco and cocoa merchants. This history of wealth is reflected in the city's magnificent examples of Victorian architecture. Explore Puerto Plata's old town with this easy stroll that will guide you through the area's proud past.

Allow: maximum 3 hours, depending on stops.

Begin the walk at the northern edge of the Parque Central on Avenida Beller.

1 Parque Central

The Parque Central is the heart of Puerto Plata and a hive of activity. The perfect place for a spot of people-watching, the green lawns and cement sidewalks are lined with carts selling sugar cane and coconuts, lottery tickets and all manner of trinkets. The central gazebo is an ideal retreat from the frenetic activity. Don't be fooled by its antique-style design – it was built in the 1960s and replicates the gazebo that stood on this spot previously.

Walk west on Beller on the northern side of the street.

The heart of the city: Parque Central

2 The Canoa

The Canoa is a treasure trove of Dominican arts and crafts. While there are many souvenir shops in the area, this is probably the best as it allows you to see the actual artists at work. Prices are on a par with most of the other shops along the Beller strip. Quality varies.

Continue west along Beller until you reach Avenida Cólon. Cross the street and go left. Your next stop is one block south of Beller on the other side of Avenida Duarte.

3 Old Immigration Centre

Once one of the grandest buildings in Puerto Plata, the old Immigration Centre is now a boarded-up, crumbling structure. There are plans to turn the place into a museum, but there is no sign of this as yet. Take a moment to admire the Immigration Centre and the Victorian warehouses that surround it for the memories they provide of a past when these vast buildings would have been filled to the brim with tropical goods on their way to the houses and factories of Europe.

Go east along Duarte on the south side of the street for approximately five blocks.

4 Catedral San Felipe

The Catedral San Felipe is one of the largest cathedrals in Puerto Plata, but its interior is not much to write home about. The exterior is the main draw, artfully combining both Art Deco and Spanish colonial influences. The interior remains locked for much of the time. Admire instead the glorious examples of Victorian architecture that line the surrounding streets.

Continue east along Duarte for two blocks.

5 Museo Ámbar

Hundreds of insects call the Museo Ámbar their last resting place, trapped as they are in the numerous amber exhibits within this two-storey museum. Located in a late 19th-century villa originally built for a German industrialist, the collection is well documented and assembled.

The second floor provides the most impressive artefacts, including dozens of pieces that have been taken from amber mines in the Cordillera Septentrional; these consist of insects, flora and fauna trapped in amber from the Jurassic and Triassic periods.

Continue east for a couple of blocks. Turn right on Eugenio Deschamps and go south for two blocks.

6 Mercado Nuevo

End your day at Puerto Plata's biggest souvenir market. Everything is mass-produced, but the energy is intoxicating. Be sure to haggle before you make any purchases.

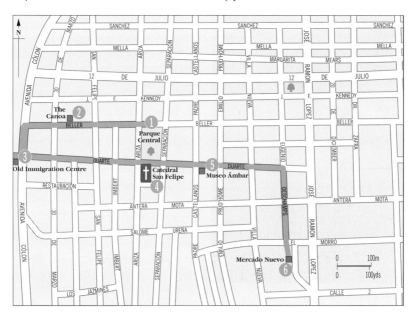

La Isabela

Site of the second established settlement formed by Christopher Columbus, La Isabela is now a national historical park. It was here on his second voyage on 29 May 1493 that Columbus arrived with 1,500 men on 17 ships.

The Templo de las Americas, La Isabela

The hardships began almost from the moment the settlers stepped off the ship. Within one week of arriving, one third of Columbus's passengers fell sick – primarily suffering from syphilis and intestinal parasites. Illness and general dissatisfaction eventually caused Columbus's fall from grace and return to Spain. In late 1494 the expedition's chief accountant led a revolt against the man Columbus left in charge in his absence – his younger brother Diego. Today, the original layout of the town can still be spotted. With a little imagination, you may be able to envisage the village that once stood on this spot.

Ruined relics

The national park and architectural excavation of La Isabela is an ongoing process. However, many of the problems faced by restorers could have been avoided years ago. Back in the 1950s, former leader Trujillo ordered that the ruins be cleaned up before he made an official visit. Unfortunately, the local militia misinterpreted his demands and bulldozed the entire site into the sea.

What to see

Excavation work on La Isabela was begun shortly after the Trujillo debacle and was speeded up in preparation for the 500th anniversary of Columbus' discovery of the New World in 1992. Stone walls mark the outlines of the main buildings, including the church in which the first Mass on American soil was read on 6 January 1494.

An underwater legacy

Erosion has caused many problems. Part of Columbus's house has fallen into the sea, a victim of more over five centuries of salt air and pounding waves. A number of wooden crosses mark the grave sites of the original inhabitants. An excavation of some of the tombs has revealed that some of the skeletons were victims of the wreck of the *Conquista*. An interesting fact to note is the way in which the dead were buried. Spanish settlers were always buried with their hands crossed. Unfortunately, everyone else wasn't as lucky. Rebels and prisoners were buried with their hands tied, to reinforce the fact that even in death they are bound by the laws of man and God. Indians would lie in an embryonic posture to highlight their perceived childlike and naïve qualities.

The national park varies in quality and authenticity. National park workers have done their best to re-establish a sense of time gone by; however, it is difficult to tell what is authentic and what is a modern-day creation. When in doubt, assume that the only genuine items from the 15th century are the foundations of each building. A variety of artefacts have been uncovered on the site, including shards of Taino and Macorix pottery and Spanish ceramics shipped over from the Old World at the time of the establishment of the settlement.

The end of the affair
La Isabela was abandoned in 1498 as the constant bouts of plague, frequent threat of hurricanes and the poor harbour finally forced the populace to look for a better location. The emigration from the

settlement must have been extremely rapid – in their hunt for relics, archaeologists have discovered a number of valuable trinkets, including cannonballs, daggers in their scabbards and entire suits of chainmail.

Parque Nacional La Isabela. Open daily 8am–5.45pm. Admission fee.
All information is provided in Spanish only. The park guides also only speak Spanish. For a detailed tour, book yourself on one of the numerous scenic trips that depart Puerto Plata with English-speaking guides.

Hidden treasures of the deep

Christopher Columbus was born around 1451 in Genoa, Italy, a region that produced some of the finest seafarers in the 15th century. He first went to sea as a teenager; his dream was to cross the Atlantic in order to find a waterway to Asia, where he hoped to locate the mythical realm of Prester John – a legendary king and priest from India whose tale of wealth and piety came to prominence in the Middle Ages. Columbus wanted to sign an agreement to export Asian goods in return for gold. After failing to convince King John II of Portugal to foot the bill for this daring venture, Columbus turned to Spain's Ferdinand and Isabella. They were engaged in trying to capture the Moorish stronghold of Granada; on its fall in January 1492 they were finally able to put their support behind Columbus. On 3 August of that year Columbus set sail with three ships: *Santa Maria*, *Niña* and *Pinta*.

Land, ahoy
After brief stops on the island of San Salvador in the Bahamas and Cuba, the admiral arrived at the north coast of Hispaniola. Columbus skirted the island's coastline, trading gold with the native Taino Indians, who told him of a mountain range located further inland known as Cibao. This mention of what is now the Dominican's heartland was mistaken for Cipango, then the European name for Japan. On Christmas Day, Columbus ran aground on a coral reef off the coast of Haiti at what is now Cap Haïtien. The explorer took this event as a sign and left 25 men to establish a settlement named La Navidad in honour of the holy event. Excited by the information from the Taino about potential gold reserves in the interior and what he thought was his proximity to Japan, Columbus returned to Spain with news of his conquest.

Laying foundations
Having listened to Columbus's reports, the Spanish royals sent him back out in late 1493 to snare more gold for their coffers – this time with a larger expedition of 1,500 men. However, on

arriving at the La Navidad settlement in 1494, Columbus found no trace of the men he had left behind. Disease or skirmishes with the Taino had resulted in their deaths. La Nueva Isabela was then founded, 100km (60 miles) further east in what is now the Dominican Republic.

The location was easily defensible, situated as it was on a cape.

Columbus was eager to establish settlements because he was convinced he was close to the great Asian civilizations and he was anxious to find them. Trading bases, modelled on the Portuguese trading posts dotted along the coast of West Africa, allowed him to barter for the gold that the Spanish crown wanted, while freeing him up to move on to other regions.

Taino trouble

Gold was considered worthless by the Taino Indians. As such, they felt no strong reason to mine for it. This proved problematic for Columbus, as it meant that he would need to stay longer than he wished in La Isabela in order to make the village profitable. Profit relied on slave labour, and the only readily available source was the local Taino tribes, which he quickly went about forcing into submission.

His troubles didn't end there, though. Malaria and yellow fever were sweeping through La Isabela with frightening strength and even the enslavement of the Taino couldn't satisfy the need for labour. Dissent spread through the settlement, culminating in the hijacking of one of Columbus's ships by a petty noble, who returned with a crew of six to Spain in protest at being asked to do manual labour. Columbus eventually had to sail for Spain in 1496 to answer charges brought against him by the dishonoured gentlemen.

Opposite top: The site of La Isabela
Opposite below: The Columbus statue in Parque Colón (Columbus Park)
Top: Columbus's name lives on all over the island, as this street sign shows
Above far left: Skeleton of a plague victim
Above left: Idealised in art

Santiago

Santiago may be the second-largest city in the Dominican Republic but, in terms of tourist numbers, it definitely ranks close to last. Situated at the gateway of the fertile Cibao region, this is a town that caters to the needs of its residents and not travellers.

Catedral de Santiago is one of the city's landmarks

A short history
Founded in 1504, Santiago has been destroyed time and time again by fire, earthquake and invasion – and yet the settlers always return. Its original *raison d'être* was as a mining town, but the fertility of Santiago's location quickly made tobacco the town's number one export. Following an invasion by the Haitians in 1805, the city was rebuilt, quickly re-establishing itself as the transport hub for tobacco heading for Puerto Plata and onwards to the Old World. Tobacco remains the primary export of Santiago, and forms the backbone of the city's economy.

Major merengue
In addition to the growth of the tobacco industry during the heyday of the 19th century, Santiago also developed as a cultural hotbed in the growth of Dominican music, specifically the '*merengue périco ripao*' – a form of the popular Dominican music style using accordion, tambora and güira. The city has produced some of the island's most famous musicians and hosts a vibrant Latin club scene.

The main sights
Santiago's most impressive sight is the Monumento a los Héroes de la Restauración de la República. Built by Trujillo to honour himself, it was re-dedicated to the soldiers who lost their lives in the War of Independence with Spain. The monument is visible from almost every point in the city.

It is possible to climb the monument to enjoy a breathtaking view of the city and – on clear days – the surrounding mountains and valleys.
Monumento a los Héroes de la Restauración, Avenida Monumental. Open: 9am–noon and 2–5pm Mon–Sat. Free.

Gran Teatro del Cibao
As a musical base, Santiago boasts a wonderful concert hall in which occasional operas and merengue concerts are staged. Built in the 1980s, this Italian marble auditorium seats 15,000 people and has amazing acoustics. Too bad the ticket prices prevent most of the local population from enjoying performances.
Gran Teatro del Cibao, Avenida Monumental. Tel: (809) 583 1150.

Museo Folklòrico de Tomas Morel
While the bright carnival masks of the town of La Vega are justifiably

renowned, you'll often find them difficult to spot out of season. Not so at this colourful museum, celebrating the papier-mâché handicrafts of the island and the Dominicans' cultural history. Inside the museum is a wonderful collection of Taino treasures, carnival masks and historical relics dating back to the 16th century. If you're looking for a bit of cultural conversation, the building also functions as an unofficial hangout for local artists, students and intellectuals.
Museo Folklòrico de Tomas Morel, Restauración 174. Tel: (809) 582 6787. Open: 9am–1pm and 3–6pm Mon–Fri. Free.

Catedral de Santiago
The cathedral is not the most beautiful of structures, but the lavender-painted concrete cathedral of Santiago, located on the southern end of the Parque Duarte, is worth checking out, if only to see the intricate mahogany carvings and contemporary stained-glass windows. The marble tomb of the 19th-century dictator Ulises Heureaux is in the sanctuary.

The huge Monumento a los Héroes dominates the city skyline

Walk:
Go Mad in the Mercado

Santiago may not be known for its sights, but when it comes to shopping, you're in the right place. The city is well known for its crafts and local produce, making it a wonderful location in which to pick up intriguing souvenirs and artistic goods.

Allow: 3 hours, including stops. You can extend the tour as suggested at the end of the walk.

Begin at Mercado Hospidaje, located on Ulisses F. Espaillat between Restauración and Independencia.

1 Mercado Hospidaje

Taking up most of the western half of downtown Santiago is the massive outdoor Mercado Hospidaje, the city's largest agricultural market. Its attraction lies in the traffic and colour around you as you meander through the chaos.

A city built on the proceeds from tobacco

Walk east along the Calle del Sol to the Parque Duarte, located on your right-hand side after you pass Bto. Monción.

2 Parque Duarte

The social heart of Santiago is pretty overcrowded, but the paths are pleasantly tree-lined and provide a cool spot in which to recharge the batteries. Horse-and-carriage rides around the city are available from here.
From the north side of the park, walk east along the Calle del Sol.

3 Museo del Tabaco

Santiago owes its life to the tobacco industry. To celebrate the power of the 'sweet leaf', the city built a museum honouring tobacco and its influence on the region since the 16th century. For more information, please see p120.
From here walk east along the Calle del Sol until you reach España.

4 Mercado Modelo Turistico

The Calle del Sol might remind you of the United States, with its American banks, low-rent shopping centres and fast-food joints. Go past all of this to reach the Mercado Modelo Turistico, a cluster of shops and booths specialising in tourist-oriented wares.

Walk south along España until you reach 16 de Agosto. Turn left and continue eastbound to the Habanera Tabaclera.

5 Habanera Tabaclera

For information, see p120.

The walk ends here. If you want to carry on shopping, you will need transport to get to points outside the centre.

6 Recommended options

The Autopista Duarte offers a range of goods, including cheap ceramics, cane furniture, fruit, vegetables and poultry. Just drive by the shops and pull over when something takes your fancy. The Bermúdez rum plant, at the corner of

Goods for sale in the market

Libertad and Armando Bermúdez in the northwest of downtown, offers private tours that include a complimentary *Cuba libre* (rum and Coke) at the end of your behind-the-scenes peek at sugar-cane processing.

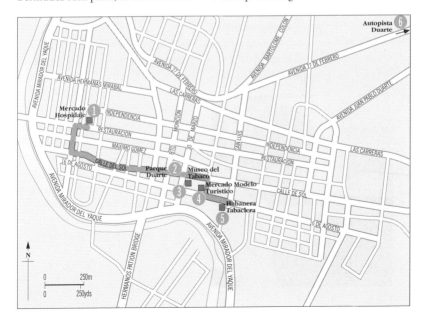

While Santiago is the second-largest city in the Dominican Republic, it boasts a much more relaxed atmosphere than the capital city to the southeast. 'Sin' forms the backbone of Santiago's economy, specifically in the form of sugarcane (to produce rum) and high-grade tobacco (for cigarettes and world-renowned cigars). As such, smokers will find many positive reasons to escape the Dominican humidity in favour of a well-stocked humidor.

Total tobacco

Before you make any purchases, consider visiting the Museo del Tabaco located on the eastern side of Parque Duarte. Opened in 1984, the museum chronicles the progression of tobacco from the 16th century (when it was first introduced to Europe) to the present day. Machinery and implements taken from actual tobacco processing plants – both past and present – are on display.

This museum will give you a good idea of the work that goes into producing just one cigar, and will show you how to differentiate between the various grades of tobacco.

Museo del Tabaco, Corner of Calle 30 de Marzo and Calle 16 de Agosto, Santiago. Open: 9am–noon, 2–5pm Tues–Fri; 9am–noon Sat.

Smoke gets in your eyes

Now that you've got an idea of the historical significance of tobacco, it's time to make a few purchases. One of the best locations in which to snag a cigar or two is at the Habanera Tabaclera, a working cigar factory located just five minutes away from the museum. The Habanera Tabaclera is reported to be the oldest continually working cigar factory in the Dominican Republic. A tour will take you through the factory floor, where you can witness the entire process of manufacturing cigars from leaf to luxury product.

Calle del Sol at the junction of San Luís and 16 de Agosto.

Please note that tours are only conducted on weekdays.

Fire sales

If you have a car and can get out of town, there is a second cigar factory known as the Tabacos Don Esteban, located 3km (2 miles) out of town on the Autopista Duarte in the direction of Santo Domingo. Tours here are a little less informative, but the purchases at the end of the tour can be slightly more affordable, especially if you buy in bulk. Quality is about the same as the Habanera Tabaclera.

Keep on rollin'

A trip northwest out of Santiago will take travellers to the towns of Navarette and Villa González, two well-known locations among cigar connoisseurs. A short drive along the Carretera Duarte will take you past wide fields of lush tobacco; these are scattered with the thatched huts used by planters to dry the leaves. A couple of cigar factories open up to the public along this stretch, conveniently located across the highway from one another – Pinar del Río Tabaclero and Túbano's. *Both are open from 8am–noon and 2–4pm Mon–Fri and are free of charge.*

For a better glimpse at the rolling practice but with fewer visitor or shopping options, consider going further west in Navarette to visit the Tabaclera Jacagua factory on the Parque Central.

Tamboril

The mecca of cigar shopping has to be the tiny town of Tamboril, found by driving 10km (6.25 miles) east on the Carretera 14 from Santiago, then 5km (3 miles) north on the Carretera Tamboril. The largest tobacco factory in town is the Flor Dominicana. It isn't tourist-friendly, so pop your head into the smaller operations clustered around the village instead. For a truly Dominican welcome, give the Fábrica Anilo de Oro on Calle Real a try.

Opposite top: A local label celebrates the leaf
Opposite below: Roll your own
Top: Cigars are enjoyed as much by locals as by tourists
Left: Hard at work: the factories are a principal source of employment in the area

Jarabacoa

Set in the heart of a region known as the 'Dominican Alps', Jarabacoa is a summer hill-resort dotted with pine forests that is popular among wealthy Dominicans. The local elite love this region of the country: the warm days and cool nights are a wonderful tonic after the oppressive heat experienced in the rest of the country during the height of summer. Visitors to the region tend to be more active types, drawn to the numerous waterfalls, rivers and mountains that are ideal for hiking and exploration.

A bridge over troubled waters in Jarabacoa

Artful lodgers

The beauty of the local landscape has drawn a number of noted sculptors and artists to Jarabacoa, many of whom offer classes and studio tours. One of the best is Roberto Flores, a professor at the Escuela de Bellas Artes in Santo Domingo. Look for examples of his work in the local church, and at the Rancho Baiguate and Rancho Restaurant. A typical Flores piece costs from US$2,000.

Rivers wild

White-water rafting and canyoning are popular pursuits for visitors to Jarabacoa. This is primarily due to the fact that three major rivers can be found flowing close to the town – the Río Jimanoa, Río Yaque del Sur and Río Baiguate. For something just as wet but less nerve-racking, a drive 10km (6.25 miles) north of town will take you to the stunning Jimenoa waterfalls. Niagara it isn't, but the lush foliage that surrounds it makes the location extremely romantic. Try and avoid the falls midday or Sundays if you don't want to wade through dozens of tour groups.

Java joy

For something a little more educational, visit the local coffee factory, Café La Joya. The entire method of production is chronicled from growing to roasting, beginning with an interesting 45-minute video illustrating the process. The tour takes you from there through the factory, where you can see hundreds of local women grading each bean for export. An obligatory gift shop at the end of the journey sells crafts and coffee products, including an absolutely delicious coffee liqueur. All proceeds benefit the local community. Tours must be arranged in advance. Bookings done through Rancho Baiguate are your best and easiest option.

Clouded over

Jarabacoa is the gateway to the Reserva Cientifica Ebano Verde, a cloud forest reserve created in 1989 to protect the green ebony tree. Information on almost every tree and path is provided, including 621 chronicled species of plants and 59 species of birds. See if you can spot '*el zumbadorcito*', which is the second smallest bird in the world, and is only found in the Dominican Republic and Jamaica.

Active adventures

There are a number of adventure tour operators based in Jarabacoa that cater to visitors looking to experience the region's wilder side. One of the best is Aventuras del Caribe. The owner, Franz Lang, is a transplanted Austrian who specializes in small-group canyoning and kayaking tours. Every level from beginner to advanced is offered, and high safety levels are always maintained.

For white-water rafting, mountain-biking, horse-riding and pretty much every other adrenaline experience, Rancho Baiguate's Aventura Máxima is another good option. The town's proximity to Pico Duarte makes Aventura Máxima a great company to consider when organising climbing expeditions. A particular advantage is that the guides and instructors who lead expeditions are both Dominican and international. This means that you get the best local knowledge combined with top-notch experience and translation services.

Aventura Máxima. Rancho Baiguate. Tel: (809) 574 4940.
Aventuras del Caribe. Tel: (809) 574 2669.

White-water rafting gets the adrenaline racing

Pico Duarte

The Caribbean's largest mountain is the Pico Duarte, the queen of the Cordillera Central. Measuring 3,087m (10,128ft) in height, the Pico Duarte towers over its smaller cousin, La Pelona ('Baldy'). Before 1930, the two peaks were known as Pelona Grande and Pelona Chica.

Pico Duarte pushes through the clouds

The area surrounding the mountain is largely uninhabited due to the serious lack of fresh water. The peak was scaled for the first time in 1944 to celebrate the 100th anniversary of Dominican independence. It was not until the 1980s, when the Dominican government built cabins and established trails, that hiking up the peak became a common occurrence. Today, approximately 3,000 people a year go up Pico Duarte in order to admire the spectacular views and sunrises from the top.

Parques Nacionales Armando Bermúdez & José del Carmen Ramírez

Parques Nacionales Armando Bermúdez and José del Carmen Ramírez are two adjoining national parks. They were designated in 1956 to prevent the massive deforestation that was happening in Haiti at the time. To witness the benefits of this forward-thinking move, you just have to look at the devastation wreaked by Tropical Storm Jeanne in 2004 when more than 2,000 Haitians lost their lives due to flooding and mudslides.

Together, these two parks contain the highest peaks in the Caribbean and they have become a popular spot for hikers, trekkers and fans of adventure travel.

Climate

As the parks are located in high altitudes, the weather here can be unpredictable. In the summer, temperatures stay at a comfortable average of 18–20°C. In the winter, however, this can drop down as far as –5°C. Rainfall is particularly high, making wet-weather clothing an absolute must. The parks receive an annual rainfall of between 2,000 and 4,000mm every year, usually in the form of pounding downpours that can cause incredible flash floods.

Going up?

Five trails take hikers up to the summit of the mountain. These are called Sabaneta, Mata Grande, Las Lagunas, Los Corralitos and – the most popular (and easiest) route – La Ciénega. Each trail is named after the town or pueblo from which the trail begins. Ranger stations exist in each of these towns, and it is here where you will have to purchase a permit that will allow you access to the park. These should not cost more than a few dollars or one or two pounds.

Everyone entering the park will also require the services of a guide. Guides can be found near the ranger stations and usually charge reasonable rates. Never try going into the park without one: the woods are very easy to get lost in and you could quickly find yourself in trouble. In any case, the eagle-eyed guides will raise the alarm if they think you are trying to get in without one.

Ranger stations are open daily from 8am to 5pm. Signed trail maps are usually posted at the stations, outlining the route of the trail and the location of cabins. Portable trail maps are, however, not common.

What to expect

While Pico Duarte is not as high as the Himalayas, the clamber up it is still quite a workout, even for experienced hikers. This is due to the quality of the trail. While large boulders and felled trees are generally cleared from the path, deep ruts are pretty much the norm. Compacted dirt gives way to loose rock, requiring sturdy ankles and a high tolerance for falling down. Proper footwear – specifically broken-in hiking boots – is a must. Not only will they protect your feet from the impact of the trail, they'll also help you keep a strong grip on the constantly shifting soil.

A choice of trails to the summit – which way to go?

Walk: Pico Duarte's La Ciénega Trail

This is the most popular trail taking hikers up the Caribbean's largest peak. You begin your journey from the quaint pueblo of La Ciénega, 25km (15.5 miles) south of Jarabacoa, where you will need to register for the 46km (28.75 miles) round-trip at the office by the park entrance. *Allow: two days of hiking and one afternoon of preparation time to complete the trail. You must be physically fit to undertake this journey.*

1 La Ciénega

Arrive at La Ciénega in the afternoon to sort out the formalities required to enter the park. After you complete the paperwork, find yourself a nice place to sleep for the night and prepare for an early start. Make sure you get provisions for the trip before arriving in La Ciénega. There are no shops or markets to speak of in the tiny hamlet.

Heading for the hills on La Ciénega

2 To Los Tablones

Walk along the trail for approximately 4km (2.5 miles) until you reach Los Tablones. This part of the journey is quite comfortable and is beautifully situated next to a river. You begin the trip in earnest when you cross a bridge.

3 Over and up

As soon as you cross the river, the adventure begins. Over the next 14km (8.75 miles), you will climb up over 2,000m (5,616ft). The track is badly eroded and requires strong hiking footwear. Make sure your boots are up to the task and have been properly worn in. Regular picnic stops along the way provide an opportunity to catch your breath. Take time to admire the woody wilderness and a spectacular view over the canopy of trees below.

4 La Comparticíon

La Comparticíon is the usual stopover point for Pico Duarte climbers. The cabins are run-down and often rat-infested (*see p127*), so use a tent if you have one. The wooden structures are usually bare, with portable toilets (use the woods instead) and sheltered grills for cooking. The cabins are free of charge.

If you plan on cooking, or if you need drinking water, make sure you boil or treat any water before you ingest it. Parasites and other nasties are common in the local creeks. Better yet, be prepared with bottled water, but ensure you do not leave any rubbish behind.

5 The final ascent

Set off from the cabin around 4.30am for the last 5km (3 miles) to the summit. Leave your belongings in one of the cabins – they should be quite safe. Ensure that you arrive on the summit in time for sunrise: the early morning rays cast a red hue over the fluffy clouds beneath you. Spend some time enjoying the panorama before backtracking down to La Ciénega – but don't forget your belongings on the way down.

RATS!

If you can avoid it, do not sleep in any of the cabins provided for unsuspecting hikers. Every night, large rats invade these dens of despair in the hope of finding food. If you think you can outsmart them, think again – these rats will chew through absolutely anything, and destroy your sleep as they do so.

If you have any food with you, the cabins are the best place to store it. If you try and zip it up in your tent or backpack and leave it on the ground, these hungry rodents will chew through them to get at it. Hanging yummies on the wall won't solve the problem either as the fat critters can climb up walls. Instead, bring a hook and hang your provisions in a plastic bag from the ceiling. Doing this will keep the rats at bay and give you the deep sleep you will be craving after a day of strenuous hiking.

The view from the summit is well worth the effort

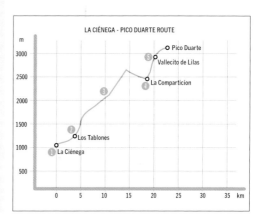

LA CIÉNEGA - PICO DUARTE ROUTE

Constanza

The town of Constanza has seen much better days. Once a popular tourist destination, it has lost most of its traffic to Jarabacoa, primarily due to that town's easy access to the trappings of Pico Duarte. It never deserved to lose its position on the tourist trail, however, situated as it is in a gorgeous, circular valley deep in the mountains.

View of the valley at Constanza

The valley was formed over a thousand years ago by a meteor. The result is a level of fertility that has beckoned farmers since the age of the Taino Indians. As the valley is more than 1,300m (3,650ft) high, it is not uncommon for the thermometer to drop below freezing in December and January.

Switzerland or sunny tropics?
As recently as the 1950s, Constanza resembled a tiny Swiss alpine village. The homes were mostly log cabins constructed from the pine trees growing on nearby slopes. Today, these homes are gone, having been replaced by cheap stucco and shantytowns. The immediate surroundings are dotted with vast plantations owned by wealthy Santo Domingans. This is the cool-climate playground of the island's rich and powerful.

What to see
Constanza's lack of success in tourism terms is due to the fact that there is almost nothing of historical importance to see: no museums, no historical buildings, no fancy restaurants or resorts. But it does have a lot of charm.

The biggest attraction is the farmers' market, located just north of the Calle Luperón. Trucks drive in, stock up and pull out with loads of local produce on the way to the supermarkets and shops of Santo Domingo. Regionally produced strawberries and raspberries are especially prized.

Japanese influences
Somewhat surprisingly, Constanza calls itself home to a sizable Japanese community. These Asian farmers arrived during the 1950s during the reign of dictator Rafael Trujillo, drawn by the promise of prime farming land at rock-bottom prices, and never left. Trujillo's goal was to transform the valley into the breadbasket of the nation – and for the most part it worked. Today, the descendants of these Asian farmers own much of the fertile land in the region.

Look for the Colonia Japonesa (Japanese Quarter), south of town. It's made up mostly of dilapidated shacks, but there is a Japanese social club on the main street that is worth seeing.

Nueva Suiza
Also located in the south of town is a former holiday home owned by the

Trujillo family. During the peak of tourist interest in the area, the manor was used as a resort spa. Today, it is fenced off from the public, boarded-up and slowly rotting. A greenhouse immediately adjacent to the building sells beautiful flowers, including roses, hyacinths and orchids.

Aguas Blancas

Constanza's major site is Aguas Blancas, a powerful, 150m (492ft) waterfall in three sections with a large pool. The trek to get here is a little tricky, but well worth the adventure. The scenery more than makes up for the difficulty.

The surrounding agricultural land is fascinating to behold. Some of the farms are perched so precariously on the mountainside that you wonder how anyone manages to ship crops into or out of the land.

To get to Aguas Blancas, drive 10km (6.25 miles) south from the Colonia Japonesa along a precarious and rocky dirt road. A four-wheel drive vehicle or a motorcycle is a must if you want to have any chance of completing the journey. Keep your eye out for the numerous grazing cows that have a tendency to stop in the middle of the road.

Workers cultivate the fields in this fertile valley

The Haitian Border Towns

Snaking along the Haitian border for more than 25km (15.5 miles), the Carretera Internacional is truly 'the road less travelled'. This difficult dirt track carves its way through the Cordillera Central, allowing travellers to see what life is like in the most remote quarters of Hispaniola.

The Dominican border

The Haitian border region was and still is the least developed region of the Dominican Republic. Getting to and through the area is extremely tricky and will require a 4WD – the roads here are little more than dirty ruts in the ground.

Dajabón

Located 20km (12.5 miles) south of Manzanillo, Dajabón is the biggest of the Haitian border towns, and one of only two locations where you can legally travel into Haiti. Due to its status as a major crossing point, Dajabón has one of the region's best Haitian markets; here you can pick up great examples of art naïf.

Until the mid-16th century, the Spanish had a fort here, but the town remained of little importance until 1794, when Toussaint L'Ouverture murdered most of the locals and resettled the location with Haitians. The river flowing along the border has been called Massacre ever since.

Market days are Mondays and Fridays from 9am until 4pm. On these days, Haitians flood the town, specifically the eight square blocks that border the bridge delineating the international border. For the best purchases, get to the market early, as the event winds down over the course of the day.

What to buy

The best buys in Dajabón are clothing and household goods shipped over from Haiti. Many of the designer labels you see for sale are actually blatant fakes, though some of them are quite well done. If you do plan on shopping, keep a firm grasp on your wallet: pickpocketing and petty theft are rife.

Fort Liberté

The border crossing at Dajabón is important from a tourist perspective because of its proximity to Fort Liberté, Haiti. Located 20km (12.5 miles) to the north of town, Fort Liberté is one of the oldest and most perfectly preserved forts in the New World. It lies ruined on the Bay of Dauphin, a circular body of water just west of the town of Fort Liberté.

Jimaní

The other 'official' Haitian border town is Jimaní. There isn't much worth stopping for in this dry, concrete town. But, if you're travelling between Santo Domingo and Port-au-Prince, this is the crossing you'll have to take.

Jimaní's Haitian market pales in comparison to the one at Dajabón. It is located just inside Haiti, once you cross the border. The area it is situated in is so bleak that it is known locally as Mal Paso ('Bad Pass'). Practical household goods provide the bulk of what is on offer here – as well as dozens of Wilson tennis balls, which are manufactured nearby.

Crossing the border

The only way to travel across the border is by foot or on a bus. Rental cars are not permitted to cross over into Haiti; insurance cover ceases to apply the second the wheels leave the Dominican. Whenever you cross, you will have to pay a US$10 Dominican departure tax (in American dollars only), a US$10 Haitian entry tax, and a US$10 Dominican entry tax when you return. Immigration is only open daily from 8am to 6pm. If you're late, you'll have to spend the night on whichever side of the border you find yourself, so keep an eye on your watch if you don't want to get caught out.

Frontier life – there is a range of products on offer in the Haitian market

Rafael Trujillo and the Haitian Massacre

In 1930, after the Americans decided to leave Dominican shores to concentrate on the economic problems in their own country, the Dominican Republic saw the rise to power of Rafael Leonidas Trujillo. Loved by some and hated by others, Trujillo formed a dictatorship so brutal that its effects still resonate through many aspects of Dominican society today – specifically in the Dominican racism against the much poorer (and usually darker) Haitians.

From his rise to power until 1961, Trujillo amassed a fortune. He controlled entire monopolies in sugar, salt, beef, rice, milk, cement, insurance and cigarettes. Family members were appointed into the highest positions in government, while 10 per cent of all public employees' salaries went directly

into his private bank accounts – to fund the political party of which he was leader. By the time his regime ended, he directly employed 60 per cent of the Dominican workforce.

The invisible border

Until Americans invaded Hispaniola in 1916, the border between Haiti and the Dominican was largely invisible, even though the boundaries had been established for more than two hundred years. Populating the centre of the island were *cimarrones*, freed black slaves who had established small subsistence farming communities.

The *cimarrones* avoided the extreme north and south near the coastline (where the border was strictly maintained) because they enjoyed the freedom of being able to pass anywhere within the island to trade their crops. The rugged interior, blanketed in thick forest, also made any policing virtually impossible.

The peaceful co-existence that had existed under this system was scattered to the wind by the US when they annexed a portion of the Sierra Barohuco largely populated by Dominicans and gave it to Haiti. They also handed over a slice of the Cordillera Central inhabited by Haitians to the Dominican Republic. They then constructed a series of dirt roads along the border to open up the interior and create a meaningful division. When the

Americans moved out, Rafael Trujillo moved in and the bloodshed began.

Genocide: Operacíon Perejil

On the night of 4 October 1937, hundreds of soldiers began the Trujillo-ordered Operacíon Perejil, ambushing a religious procession to the Cave of San Francisco outside the town of Bánica. Hundreds of Haitians who had crossed the border to worship were killed. The soldiers separated the Dominicans from the Haitians by demanding that each person in the crowd should say the word *perejil* ('parsley'), which native Kreyol-speakers find difficult to pronounce. The Dominicans were told that the captives had been sent to deportation centres to be 'processed'. In reality, the Haitians were taken out at night, hacked to death with machetes and fed to the sharks in the Bahía de Manzanillo.

Over the next two months the killings continued as the police force murdered as many Haitians as they could identify living in the Dominican Republic. In that time 20,000 to 25,000 Haitian peasant farmers living on the Dominican side of the border were exterminated. The Dominican government later paid the Haitian government US$525,000 in reparations.

Post-massacre politics

Relations with Haiti have remained extremely frosty right up to today. Many of the Dominican border towns were given new, suitably patriotic names, like Restauración or Villa Anacaona, to serve as a daily reminder to Haitians of their perceived inferiority. Thousands of Haitians still attempt to cross the border every year to harvest the annual sugar-cane crop; nevertheless the racism against them continues.

Opposite: Haitians still suffer persecution
Top: The Mirabal sisters, who opposed Trujillo's regime and were murdered
Left: The deadly dictator, Trujillo

Lago Enriquillo

Stunningly beautiful and absolutely enormous, Lago Enriquillo is a shallow saltwater lake that is 42km (26 miles) long and 12km (7 miles) wide. The water is actually three times saltier than the sea because of steady evaporation. While swimming is a little unpleasant due to the high salinity, the bed is covered with a thick layer of ancient shells and fossilised coral – if you can open your eyes long enough to look, that is.

Lakeside living in La Descubierta

Lake Enriquillo is the lowest point in the Caribbean, lying at the bottom of a natural basin almost 40m (130ft) below sea level. As such, the region is very hot and dry, yet it remains extremely fertile thanks to the numerous springs and small rivers that dot the landscape. Temperatures here can be as much as 9°C higher than in the towns that line the coast.

Beware of crocodiles

Following the ring road

One of the easiest ways to see the lake is to follow the loop road that runs all the way around it. The journey is popular amongst wealthy Dominicans. It is not uncommon to see families packed into cars to enjoy the views or picnicking along the shores of the lake. Driving here is slow-going, due both to the quality of the road and the slow-moving vehicles – but you don't let that annoy you. This is definitely not a place you want to rush through.

The most convenient place from which to start your trip is Barahona (*see p140*). Leave the town along Carretera 44 in a northwesterly direction. After 12km (7 miles), take the turnoff for the Carretera 48 to the left, across the Río Yaque del Sur. If you enjoy the sight of acres of sugar cane growing in the fields, you'll enjoy this portion of the journey. Go past the minuscule village of Tamayo and then cross the foothills of the Sierra de Neiba until you reach your first stop, the town of Neiba. Your entire journey around the lake is along the 48, so as long as you stick to the highway, you'll eventually find yourself back at the junction with the 44 from which you started.

Neiba

Neiba is a friendly market town that specialises in the production of extremely sour grapes. You'll know if the grapes are in season if you head over to the market square in the centre of town. If the harvest is in, then the square will be covered in them.

In terms of sights, the town is pretty limited, though there is a cold sulphur spring about 2km (1.25 miles) east of town. Otherwise, Neiba should be considered only as a good stopping point if you need to rest your head for the night. The town is a popular pit stop for cross-country *gua-gua* (long-distance bus) drivers going into Haiti or travelling long distances in the Dominican.

Enriquillo's secret lair

Above the road near Postrer Río are a series of caves, some of which bear witness to the past presence of Taino Indians. The ascent is strenuous and not suitable for anyone who is not physically fit: it's a climb of about 50m (140ft) over steep, rough terrain. Inside the caves are a number of intriguing scratches resembling faces. Some of the scratches

The saltwater shores of Lago Enriquillo

are more 'artistic' than others, but give you a sampling of native culture. It is thought that the caves were once a hideout for the great Indian leader Enriquillo (*see p38*), during the period when he was fighting the Spaniards. It's not hard to picture him seated just inside the entrance, keeping watch over the land below. The view stretches for miles, and is an excellent position from which to view the whole of the lake.

Isla Cabritos
The largest of the three islands in the lake is Isla Cabritos, or the 'Isle of Goats', as it is known in English. Due to its remoteness, Cabritos has been turned into something of a natural paradise, supporting an abundance of wildlife. Giant iguanas, alligators and a pink mass of flamingos all call this island home.

The best way of getting to the island is with one of the organised tours that depart from the park entrance located 4km (2.5 miles) east of La Descubierta, near the lake's northwestern tip. Not only is this the cheapest and easiest way of getting there, it's also the most exciting, as guides have been known to get into the water and steer the boat 'up close' to the numerous American alligators.

Boats leave daily at 7.30am, 8.30am and 1pm – although this schedule is dependent on demand and is liable to change at a moment's notice. Always check in advance in order to avoid disappointment. The journey from the mainland takes approximately 45 minutes and should cost between RD$100 and RD$1,000, depending on the size of your party.

The actual island is extremely arid and sandy. Covered with cactus, Cabritos is well-known for the large numbers of half-tame rhinoceros iguanas, which will crowd around you in hopes of being fed. Please don't do it. Feeding them only encourages their reliance on man, and many types of food are extremely bad for them.

La Descubierta
One of the larger outposts on the Lago ring road is La Descubierta. A rather sleepy little town, La Descubierta is something of a green oasis, situated as it is in one of the most arid parts of the country. The town owes its health to the cold sulphur spring, located in the nearby area of Las Barías. If you're hot and tired from all the driving, the spring is an excellent place to cool down and meet the locals. You will join in a hive of activity as children splash around in the cooling liquid, women wash their clothes, and seniors chat away under the shade of the palm trees. If you're hungry, grab a bite from the nearby palm-roofed kitchen by the shore.

If you like to ramble, there are a couple of short paths through the forest that wind between Las Barías and La Descubierta. Shaded as it is by the oak trees that surround it, the walk is actually quite cool, offering some protection from the power-sapping sun that bakes the region.

Laguna del Rincon
The Carretera 46 is the main road that hugs the southern shore of Lago Enriquillo. Just before you reach Duvergé on the left is the tiny village –

little more than two houses and a chicken – of La Zurza. Continue 5km (3 miles) beyond the village and there will be a turning to Neiba and the beginning of your tour.

At the junction of the two roads is an extremely imposing memorial to the Taino leader Enriquillo (*see pp38–9*), who was considered by many to be the first great fighter for independence in the New World.

Continue past Mella in the direction of Cabral. Just before you get there, you will see the Laguna del Rincon on the left-hand side. Five metres deep, the Laguna is a freshwater lake extending across an area of 30sq km (11.5sq miles). As the second largest lake in the country, it is home to a vast number of

flamingos, cormorants and turtles. From here, the major city of the region, Barahona, is just a few miles away.

Desolate yet beautiful, Lago Enriquillo is 40m (131ft) below sea level

Parqué Nacional Jaragua

Parqué Nacional Jaragua is the largest national park in the country. It is also, perhaps, the most inviting, if you are attracted by the idea of untouched beaches glowing with golden sand and lapped by the crystal-hued Caribbean. Sounds inviting? It should do.

One of the many residents of Jaragua Park

The Parqué Nacional Jaragua covers the entire southern part of the Barohuco peninsula, including two secluded islands located just off the coast: Isla Beata and Alto Velo.

While the park is absolutely massive, it's also probably one of the Dominican's best-kept secrets. This is primarily because you can only enter if you obtain a permit from the central park administration in Santo Domingo. You must also hire a guide. This is obviously not a viable option for the backpacker on a budget.

Flora and fauna

A dedicated nature reserve, the park is filled with palm trees, cactuses and several caves. These may look ripe for exploration, but you should only go in if you have a guide with you to show you around. This is not a place in which to get lost.

In terms of plant and animal life, you will really feel you have hit the jackpot here. The flora and fauna are incredibly varied, and more than half of all bird species native to the island can be found here, including the almost extinct Hispaniola buzzard.

If you're lucky, you may even spot a rare turtle or two.

Pedernales

A good jumping-off point for the park is the town of Pedernales. From the town, Jaragua is an easy drive via a well-marked turnoff that is located 12km (7.5 miles) east. Pedernales is also the best point from which to hire boats to take you to Isla Beata and Alto Velo. Both islands are well worth visiting if you have the time.

The ultimate in untouched

While a visit to the islands of Isla Beata and Alto Velo is incredibly difficult to organise, you will quickly realise – once you get to your destination – that the expense, time and hassle was well worth it.

Tell your captain to visit Beata first. On first glance, you may find the island desolate, with only scrub-brush and guano-covered rock formations greeting you. However, if you disembark your craft on the south coast, explorations will take you to a series of caves decorated with Taino rock art. These are probably the most striking and best-preserved examples anywhere in the Dominican Republic.

Alto Velo is much smaller than Beata. It is extremely rocky and surrounded by almost frighteningly deep blue water.

The island recently gained a level of scientific notoriety when the world's smallest lizard – the Dwarf Gecko, measuring just 1.6cm (half an inch) across – was found to populate its shores.

A word of warning, though: if you are prone to seasickness, it is best to think twice before tackling this trip. The journey can be extremely rocky and can take anywhere from three to five hours, depending on the power and size of your boat. Make sure your captain fills the gas tank up to allow for a full day's journey, and be prepared to fork out at least RD$1,200 to ensure that this is done – or you might find yourself stranded in paradise.

OBTAINING PARK PERMITS

Park permits can be ordered through the Direccíon Nacional de Parques. The red tape, like most things involving the Dominican government, can take a while, so be sure to budget at least a day to fill out and obtain the necessary paperwork. The parks administration is also your source for approved guides. Order your guide at the same time as you obtain the permit, or you could find yourself stranded at the park gates with no possible way of being let in.

Direccíon Nacional de Parques, Avenida Independencia, Santo Domingo. Tel: (809) 221 4104.

Spectacular cacti are among the varied flora and fauna

Barahona

Of all the locations in the Dominican Republic that are considered tourist-focused, Barahona is by far the most untouched. Unfortunately, the one part that has been affected by man is the beach – the town's entire coastline is blighted by a large mining operation.

The fire station plaque at Barahona

Barahona is best thought of as a base for exploring the Península de Pedernales, and a relatively big base at that. Just over 90,000 people call the city home, drawn by an economy based largely on sugar-cane farming and bauxite mining.

Until the eyesore known as Barahona's beach is dismantled, tourist development is likely to remain at relatively low levels.

A Haitian history

In Dominican terms, the city of Barahona is young. Founded in 1802 by the Haitian General Toussaint l'Ouverture, Barahona became the unofficial capital of Toussaint's booming sugar industry. Toussaint intended the port to become an alternative stopping point to Santo Domingo, which is located approximately 160km (100 miles) to the west.

Toussaint's dream hasn't exactly stood the test of time. While the port still imports and exports large quantities of salt, wood, wax, larimar and agricultural produce, it does not have half the power of the capital city.

The cost of corn

The city can trace the loss of its economic muscle to one important historical moment – the development of US-manufactured corn syrup. The United States, keen to reduce its dependence on imported sugar, turned to high-fructose corn syrup instead of sugar in the early 1970s. Corn syrup provided all the taste benefits of sugar, but cost a lot less to produce. That, combined with the slowly spiralling price of sugar, has turned Barahona from a city with a future to one that reminisces about its past.

Towards tourism

To take the sting away from the destruction of the sugar industry, Barahona is turning towards tourism as a way of getting out of the economic doldrums. Luckily the location of the town is simply stunning.

Protected from the open sea by reefs, the beaches that surround Barahona are superb. The crowds you might experience in resorts like Playa Dorada and Boca Chica do not materialise here. In the 17th century, the secluded setting of the Bay of Neiba, on which the town is located, was a favourite resting stop for pirates. Virtually inaccessible by land, this plot of land served as a safe haven for far-from-saintly sailors. The notorious Robin Hood-figure Cofresí, famous for having terrorised ships from America and Europe in the 1820s, is even thought to have hidden here at one point during his illustrious career.

What to see

In terms of sights, Barahona isn't exactly brimming with options. While the wooden houses are quaint and worth a rustic picture or two, they have not been well maintained. Even the church – traditionally the focal point of every Dominican town – has been left to rot.

If you enjoy people-watching, check out the Parque Central. Several restaurants and a disco line the park: it is definitely where Barahona's various segments of society gather. Whatever time of the day you visit, you can usually find a cluster of friendly locals wandering through. You may, however, want to avoid night-time explorations unless accompanied.

The Barahona highlight

To truly understand why Barahona is so

The rugged but beautiful southwest coast

special, you will need to contemplate its location. Barahona is situated in a glorious position at the top of the Península de Pedernales, giving easy access to the nearby national parks.

If panoramas are what you are after, drive high into the mountains of the Sierra de Bahoruco, where you can bask in the glow of some of the Dominican's most splendid scenery. For sun, sea and sand, you'll need to make a journey south in order to discover what the Côte d'Azur must have looked like before millions of pampered tourists descended on it.

Outside the city

Beyond Barahona, the coast is immaculate. A newly paved coast ride winds alongside the glistening Caribbean at the foothills of the Bahoruco Mountains. A few minutes' drive will bring you to palm-tree dusted stretches of sand that are practically deserted.

For a truly special spot, drive 10km (6 miles) south along the coast road and take a left turn towards the Playa El Quemaito. Follow the road for another 20km (12 miles) until you reach the

Busy in Barahona

Playa San Rafael. At this magical spot, a small freshwater stream meets the sea. Choose between splashing around in either fresh- or saltwater, and afterwards treat yourself to some deliciously cooked fish from the wooden huts.

Quenaito

If you would prefer to experience a few more trappings of the type usually associated with the term 'resort', head south from Barahona along Highway 44 to Quenaito. A couple of small hotels are set near this 'developed' beach. The Casablanca hotel is worth stopping off at. While the actual rooms are rustic (to say the least), the grounds are perfect for a stroll. Enjoy the view of the beach below from the cliffside where the property is located. Try to time your visit to coincide with dinner. The owner of the hotel is a gourmet French chef who was once editor-in-chief of a European cooking magazine. You won't find cuisine like this anywhere else in the region.

Lovely larimar

The Península de Pedernales, on which Barahona is situated, is the region known for the production of larimar. Mines are dotted throughout the area, and some of them can be visited – although do not expect anything fancy. Because larimar is only native to the Dominican Republic, larimar mines are constantly in operation and usually located far from the nearest road.

The most convenient mine to visit is near the tiny pueblo of Arroyo. It is hard to get to, but worth checking out if you are interested in geology. Arroyo is located 5km (3 miles) southwest of Quenaito through the rainforested Sierra Bahoruco.

However, do not attempt the journey if it has rained recently. The only way to reach the mines is down a dirt turnoff at the cockfighting arena. There is then a further drive of 8km (5 miles) through lush rainforest. The dirt road turns into a pile of impassable mud after rain, and a 4WD vehicle is an absolute must at all other times of the year. Raw chunks of the stones are available from the miners if you are looking for an intriguing souvenir. Go a further 100m (328ft) or so down the road and you will come across a river with a small waterfall –

a sublime spot in which to cool down after the tough trek.

WHO IS MARIA MONTEZ?

For a region this sparse, it may come as a bit of a surprise that there is an airport to service the community. The Aeropuerto Maria Montez is named for the Barahona-born Hollywood actress who made a name for herself in the 1940s. The Dominican darling starred in more than 20 films – mostly in ethnic roles. Two of Montez's cinematic successes were *The Arabian Nights* and *Ali Baba and the Forty Thieves*.

Beautiful blue larimar for sale

Shopping

Shopping in the Dominican Republic can be a bit hit or miss. On the one hand, the country boasts fine examples of jewellery made from amber (*see p148*) and larimar – a blue stone unique to the island. On the other hand, shopping isn't really the main reason why people visit the country. For every beautiful example of art and craftsmanship, you'll find a souvenir shop specialising in tops that say 'My mother/sister/aunt/best friend went to the Dominican Republic and all I got was this lousy T-shirt'. It can be enough to make anyone despair.

Artwork on sale on the Dominican streets

To enjoy your shopping experience in the Dominican, it is best to go into it with an open mind and a sense of fun – and not as if you are attacking London's Oxford Street on Christmas Eve. Get your bartering skills in order and don't be afraid to say no. Salespeople in resort towns and the roaming vendors who congregate on the beach may get aggressive, but if you give them a firm no, they will eventually get the hint.

Cigars

Casa Francia Cigar Shop
Follow the process of cigar-making from leaf to match in this small shop dedicated to supporting things that go up in smoke.
Vicioso 103, Santo Domingo. No telephone. Open: 9am–5pm Mon–Sat.

Cigar King
The place isn't cheap, but it is the most respected supplier of stogies in the country. Almost all the well-known Dominican and Cuban brands are stocked.

El Conde 458, Santo Domingo. Tel: (809) 689 2565. Open: 9.30am–12pm, 2.30–5.30pm Mon–Sat.

Cohiba Hecho a Mano
A branch of the famous cigar manufacturer. An on-site cigar roller will even teach you how to roll your own.
El Conde 109, Santo Domingo. Tel: (809) 685 6425. Open: 9am–6pm Mon–Sat.

Cuevas y Hermanos Fabricantes de Cigarros
Amazing Dominican cigars at factory prices. Cuevas y Hermanos manufacture cigars for a number of other brands. The La Perla Habana label often sells Cuevas cigars under their own label. It's a bit like buying designer goods that have had the tag taken out. It is the same high-quality product; you just don't get bragging rights. You will, however, brag about the savings of almost 50 per cent. If you are considering a major purchase, you can try a sample for free before you close the deal.
Calle San Felipe 29, Puerto Plata.

Tel: (809) 586 7983. Open: noon–10pm Mon–Sat.

Larimar

The Canoa

If you want to get an idea of the detail and craftsmanship that goes into making your piece of larimar jewellery, then check out the factory at the back of this shop. There are usually two or three artisans at work throughout the day and they are more than happy to show off their talents. Good quality Haitian art in the primitive style is also available. All prices are negotiable.

Calle Beller near Calle 3 de Marzo, Puerto Plata. No telephone. Open: 9am–6pm Mon–Sat.

Las Indias Gift Shop

Good quality larimar and amber pieces. Prices are open to negotiation.

Arzobispo Meriño near El Conde, Santo Domingo. No telephone. Open 9am–5pm Mon–Sat.

Museo Larimar Dominicano

Huge selection of good-quality larimar products in a variety of prices and styles.

Isabela La Católica, Santo Domingo. Tel: (809) 689 6605. www.larimarmuseum.com Open: daily 9am–6pm.

Plenty of colourful Dominican clothes to catch the eye

Religious and souvenir items jostle for position

The Swiss Mine

Positively the finest boutique in Santo Domingo for buying jewellery made from larimar or amber. The shop is owned and operated by a Swiss team, and the quality and authenticity of each item in the shop is guaranteed. The workmanship put into every piece is unmatched anywhere else in the country. You'll probably pay about a third to a quarter less than you might back home. If you want to make a big purchase of jewellery, this is the place to make it.

El Conde 101, Santo Domingo. Tel: (809) 221 1897. Open: 9am–7pm Mon–Sat; 9am–4pm Sun.

Music
Karen CD Store

Music outlet for the Dominican recording company, Karen, that made stars out of a number of Dominican singers, including Juan Luis Guerra. Be warned that they only stock music by Karen performers.
El Conde 251, Santo Domingo. Tel: (809) 686 0019. Open: Mon–Sat 9am–6pm.

Musicalia

A positive mecca for fans of merengue and its offshoot *bachata*. The selection of oldies and much-loved native Dominican performers is beyond compare.
El Conde 464, Santo Domingo. No telephone. Open: 9am–6pm Mon–Sat.

Native Art

El Mamey

Authentic carnival masks from La Vega. A unique, if slightly awkward-to-carry, gift for the folks back home.

Isabela 110, Santo Domingo. Tel: (809) 689 0236. Open: 9.30am–12pm, 2.30–5.30pm Mon–Sat.

Elin Gallery

The finest collection of Haitian paintings in the Dominican Republic. Expect to pay about half what you would normally do back home. Don't let the presentation of the works dissuade you from making a purchase. While the paintings may be stacked along the walls, this is the place to come if you are serious about purchasing.

Meriño 203, Santo Domingo. Tel: (809) 688 7100. Hours vary. Phone ahead to check.

Galería Toledo

Excellent selection of Haitian primitives. A variety of carnival masks from La Vega are also available. Probably the best place to go if you are serious about Caribbean art.

Isabel La Católica 163, Santo Domingo. Tel: (809) 689 7649. Open: 9.30am–12noon, 2.30–5.30pm Mon–Sat.

MERCADO MAGIC

If you want to have a real Dominican shopping experience, then head down to the local *mercado*, or market. Every city and town in the country has one, whether it is held every day – like the ones in Puerto Plata and Santo Domingo – or infrequently in rural communities. Everything from food to basic clothes to appliances is on sale in these monuments to capitalism. Sometimes, you can even find an antique treasure – but you'll have to hunt for it. To find the location and opening times of the market in the town you are visiting, either ask your hotel concierge or a local. They will be happy to point you in the right direction.

Designer goods for sale in this modern shopping centre

What is amber?

Amber is fossilised resin produced by trees millions of years ago. Way back before the dawn of man, trees carpeted the Dominican island. At some point, these trees fossilised, hardening the sap within to form amber.

Dominican amber is considered the finest in the world. Most amber from the Dominican Republic can be dated back as far as 25 million years. Some types can only be found in the country, specifically blue amber. Dominican amber is particularly prized for the quality of its colour and the large number of inclusions – frogs, lizards and insects – that can be found trapped inside. The greater the number of inclusions, the greater the value of the amber.

Which colour to choose?

Red Dominican amber is warmer than that found in the Baltics. A good quality piece will positively glow when brought into sunlight. Yellow amber is about as good as the similar amber found in

Egypt, but features more inclusions and is therefore more highly valued. Even more expensive is black amber. The oldest form of amber you can buy on the island, black amber is also the rarest. Lack of resources means even small pieces made from black amber will cost a fortune.

What to avoid

Amber scams are rife in the Dominican Republic. Because of the country's established presence as an amber producer, many con artists have developed numerous tricks to part you from your hard-earned cash. One of the most common practices is to switch amber for common plastic. This is an easy scam to avoid if you know what to look for.

Four easy ways to determine if the amber you are looking at is the real thing:

1 Drop the amber in a glass of salted water. If the specimen floats, then it's real.

2 Rub the amber against wool or cotton. Amber acquires static electricity.

3 Hold a match to the amber. If the smell is warm and natural, then it's real. Anything chemical in odour is obviously fake.

4 Illuminate the amber with fluorescent light. If the glow changes then it is amber. If it doesn't, then you're holding a chunk of plastic.

If the dealer you are negotiating with is reputable, they should have a fluorescent light on hand to allow customers to test the merchandise.

Where to buy it?

If you want to play it safe, make your purchase from a reputable dealer. Beach vendors, while inexpensive, are probably

offering you something made from the same substance as a Barbie doll. Some of the Dominican's best amber vendors include:

Galería de Ámbar
Calle 12 de Julio near Calle José del Carmen Ariza, Puerto Plata. Tel: (809) 586 2101. www.finegiftcc.cjb.net.

Museo de Ámbar
El Conde 107, Santo Domingo. Tel: (809) 221 1333.

Museo de Ámbar
Corner of Calle Emilio Prud'homme and Duarte, Puerto Plata. Tel: (809) 320 8714. www.ambermuseum.com

Museo Mundo de Ámbar
Meriño 452, Santo Domingo. Tel: (809) 682 3309.

Opposite top: An amber bonanza
Opposite below: An insect in amber
Top: Stalls sell amber goods, but do test their authencity before buying
Left: A stunning necklace

Entertainment

When it comes to finding something to do at night, your choices are decidedly limited, especially if you are not in the capital city. As it is a financially challenged country, the Dominican Republic does not have the resources to fund national arts institutions like other neighbouring countries. But that does not mean to say that there is no culture here.

Expert dancers teach tourists the merengue

High culture
While the Dominican Republic cannot be flash with its cash, it does manage to find the resources to fund a ballet, symphony and opera. While the companies aren't exactly of the best quality, the artists try their hardest and deserve a lot more support than they actually get. You can

Drums provide an essential backbeat

catch performances at the Teatro Nacional in Santo Domingo.

The theatre is an absolutely stunning piece of white-marble architecture, built following the assassination of the dictator Trujillo in 1961. Trujillo willed the land that the building was constructed on. There are also four museums and a library in the same block of real estate.
Teatro Nacional, Plaza de la Cultura, Santo Domingo. Tel: (809) 682 7255.

Dance till you drop
Resort towns are usually a bit more action-packed. Every major tourist destination will have at least two discos that play pop hits, salsa and merengue. All-inclusive resorts will also have private discos designated for guests. However, discos in the all-inclusive resorts tend to lack the character and energy of the venues located in town. They also play a greater percentage of English-language hits.

I hear music
Live music is a way of life in the Dominican. Whether it's a simple guitar

player strolling on the Malecón or a seven-piece Latin dance band, you can pretty much guarantee that you'll hear a tune or two at some point during your day. Better-quality restaurants often book bands in to entertain guests – usually on the slower days of the week. Most live music will be Latin ballads, salsa or merengue, although there are a few themed restaurants in the country that even play Middle Eastern folk music and German oom-pah-pah. If you want to enjoy a romantic night out on the town, think twice before you book yourself into a dining spot that features live music. Very often, the manager is of the opinion that the louder the music, the better the atmosphere. It is best then to ask for a table well away from the stage or dance floor if you want to avoid a perforated eardrum.

Strolling the Malecón

You might think that it shouldn't be listed as entertainment, but if you truly want to do as the locals do, then you will schedule a night or two for strolling down the town's main beachside road, or Malecón. In a seaside community, the Malecón acts as the social heart of town. It is here that lovers court, bars hug the pavement and musicians entertain the masses. There's bound to be a bench or two to park yourself on, but if you really want to have a good time, sit down at a café and watch the people go by.

A La Vega carnival mask

THE CAR WASH

Dominican nights will see most locals hanging around the local 'car wash'. Before you panic, it's not what you think. A car wash is a bar/disco that acts as both the main centre to gossip and the place to dance and romance. They are called car washes because they are usually owned by Dominicans who have returned from the United States with money in their pocket, hoping to open a fancy car wash. Instead they settle for opening a watering hole. If you want to know where you should hang out, go to the outskirts of any small town and look for the sign that says 'Car Wash'.

If you want to really get into the soul of a Dominican, then you should listen to a merengue. By far the most popular form of music in the country, merengue is a form of dance music. It features a beat pattern that hits firmly on the first and third beat.

Compared to other Latin dance and music forms like salsa and mambo, merengue may seem haphazard and lacking syncopation. The key to understanding the form is to listen to the patterns that weave through the rhythm section.

Depending on who you are listening to, a merengue can sound modern (contemporary keyboards, saxophones and trumpets) or traditional (piano, bass and accordion). No matter what the instrumentation is like, you can always count on a strong percussion section of *congas*, *tamboras* (a two-sided lap-drum that is rapped with a stick), bass drum and *güira* (a kitchen utensil of any form that represents the influence of the Taino Indians who first populated the island).

At first listen, you may not like the quality of singing in a merengue. Vocalists tend to be very nasal. If they get it right, however, the effect can be enchanting. Singers to look out for include Johnny Ventura and John Luís Guerra.

Merengues are popular in the Dominican because they serve as a type of music people can romance and dance to, but they are also used as political satire. In many cases, a dance to a merengue may be a person's only outlet against a system that keeps them poverty-stricken and lacking any real power. Lyrics often have double meanings. So if you think you're dancing to a romantic number and everyone starts laughing, you might want to question who the singer is really talking about.

While it isn't exactly clear where the merengue comes from, most anthropologists feel that the dance form may have its origins in Haiti. African

drum-beats pervade the music; there was also a music form known as mereng that was popularised by the mulatto classes of Haiti in the 18th century. The music crossed the border as Haitians fled the constant battles and internal strife that plagued the nation through the 19th and early 20th centuries. Initially, the Catholic Church took a dim view of the dance craze, feeling it was too African and that it caused dancers to work up too much of a sexual fervour. Rural Dominicans loved the music, however, and continued to dance their cares away, despite the cultural prejudices of the upper classes.

Today, merengue is enjoyed by one and all. You can even find all-inclusive resorts offering daily classes to help you strut your stuff. If you want to experience the real thing, your best option is to hit the dance floor at a traditional merengue dance hall. A selection of some of the best are listed below:

Guácara Taína

Avenida Mirador del Sur 655, Santo Domingo. Tel: (809) 530 2662. Open Thursday–Sunday.

Las Palmas Bar

Corner of Avenida Independencía and Abraham Lincoln, Santo Domingo. Tel: (809) 221 1511. Closed Sunday.

Merengue Bar

Malecón 367, Renaissance Jaragua Hotel, Santo Domingo. Tel: (809) 221 2222.

Vieja Havana

Avenida Máximo Gómez, Santo Domingo. No telephone. Thursdays and Sundays only.

Top: Moving to a merengue beat
Opposite: Maracas for the merengue rhythm

A feast of fun in the children's museum

Children

Dominicans love their children and treat them like the little treasures they are. Children are permitted in all but the most luxurious of restaurants, and will be catered for – especially in the major resort towns.

All-inclusive solutions

Most families who visit the Dominican Republic stay at an all-inclusive resort. These properties have plenty of activities for little ones of all ages, and good childcare facilities for those periods when you want to spend some time away from the children.

Staying healthy

The Dominican sun is extremely strong, so if you are sending the kids out for the day, ensure you slap on plenty of waterproof sunblock with a minimum SPF of 25. Reapply throughout the day. A floppy hat and long sleeves will provide additional protection.

Children should only ever drink bottled water here – and they should only brush their teeth using bottled water as well. Waterborne diseases are extremely nasty in this part of the world, especially on delicate stomachs.

Legalities

Legally, children who are accompanied by only one of their parents can only stay in the Dominican Republic for a maximum of 30 days. This is an important factor to take into consideration if you are planning an extended stay and are divorced or separated from your spouse. Officials are unlikely to give you any leeway or visa extensions should your plans change.

Children who are not accompanied by a parent must have a notarised permit from the Dominican embassy or consulate in their home nation.

Be careful

If you are not staying in a resort and your children want to go off swimming, it is a good idea to watch them at all times. The currents off the Dominican coast vary wildly. Some beaches may be completely placid, while others feature dangerous undertows. City beaches usually have at least one lifeguard on duty to protect the public, but if you are somewhere secluded, then you are on your own. It's a good idea to test the waters yourself before you allow your child anywhere near them – though make sure you are careful too.

Because so many resorts are cordoned off from the general public, Dominican children rarely get a chance to meet children from other nations. If you are staying at an all-inclusive resort, there will be absolutely no chance for your offspring to mix with other children from the country. So, if you want your children to experience a wider world, factor in a day or two out of your itinerary to enjoy the public beaches in the area – though make sure you keep your eye on your children at all times.

Keeping them occupied

If you are looking for child-focused entertainment centres and museums, you may be out of luck. There are no amusement parks or funfairs in the Dominican Republic. With so many all-inclusive resorts packed with activities, this sort of entertainment has not been developed. The cultural museums in Santo Domingo can be good for an hour of Taino Indian lore, but the uninspiring displays may bore the children fast.

A better destination to include is Santo Domingo's Zona Colonial. The quaint shops are packed with goods that your kids will be enticed by, while the pirate legends of the area will do much to spark their imaginations.

FUSSY EATERS

Unless you are in a tourist resort, kids' menus can be hit and miss. Beach towns frequented by foreigners will offer menus of the types of meals that your children may be more familiar with, but if your youngster is a fussy eater and you are away from the main resorts, there may not be many dishes that appeal.

A cooling treat for those hot days

Sport and Leisure

Baseball may be considered America's national pastime, but for the Dominican Republic it is an unofficial national religion. Dominican baseball stars fill the rosters of many of the teams in America's big leagues. Sammy Sosa and George Bell are just a couple of stars who hailed originally from this island nation.

Mountain biking in the Cordillera Septentrional

Baseball

The season runs from October to January, but you can pretty much guarantee that you'll see some form of the sport played year-round, whether by kids in the city streets or by adults in the various baseball stadiums scattered throughout the country.

Every major city boasts at least two teams – one amateur and one professional – and you can count on all tickets being sold out well in advance of game day. Don't worry if you haven't pre-booked, as there are always 'scalpers' or 'touts' selling tickets outside the stadiums, though these may come at a price. Before you resort to paying top dollar, check with your hotel concierge or favourite taxi driver. You never know what connections they might have, and the overall payout is likely to be far cheaper. Ticket prices vary: the cheapest seats (around US$2) will give an obstructed view past the outfield and top price will be for a seat behind home plate. Touts will charge a premium for tickets to an important match.

Basketball

The Dominican Republic has a highly competitive basketball team that has done very well in years past, at both the Olympics and the World Championships. Many American players come to the Dominican Republic in the hopes of being spotted by an NBA scout. Games are played all year at the Centro Olímpico in Santo Domingo. Tickets are free and do not need to be reserved beforehand.

Cockfighting

Weekends are cockfighting days in almost every town and city in the country. You can guarantee that, even if you're in the middle of nowhere, you'll find a *gallera* (cockfighting pit) a few steps away. If you're squeamish, cockfighting isn't the sport for you – it's bloody and puts the animals through a lot of pain. If you want a truly authentic Dominican experience, however, the carnivalesque atmosphere of drinking, betting and yelling is incomparable. In Santo Domingo, fights occur at the Coliseo Galístico de Santo Domingo on Avenida Luperón.

Golf

With so many resorts on the Dominican Republic, it should not come as a surprise that there are also plenty of golf

Horse riding with a beach view

courses. The three best are at Casa de Campo in La Romana, Playa Dorada and Playa Grande on the Silver Coast. The most affordable courses are at Playa Dorada and Playa Grande, where green fees will set you back RD$450. The Teeth of the Dog course at Casa de Campo might require a second mortgage, with green fees at around US$125. US dollars are the only currency accepted at the 'Teeth of the Dog' course.

Mountain biking

While bicycling on an ordinary machine in the Dominican Republic will send you to an early grave, the Cordillera Septentrional is justifiably renowned for its mountain-biking opportunities. Cabarete is the place to go to arrange mountain-bike rentals or to book an excursion. Itineraries can last from a day to a week, depending upon how challenged you want to be.

Food and Drink

Dominican cuisine is a mix of Spanish, African and Taino influences, blended into what locals call *cómida criolla*. Rice and beans – red beans or small black beans known as *morros* – are mainstays of the Dominican diet. Chicken is the most popular main course, and it can be served grilled or fried, or as a soupy sauce known as *asopao*. Plantains are another basic, served as a side dish with almost every meal.

Fresh from the country, fruit and vegetables galore

Breakfasts

Traditional Dominican breakfasts were designed for farmworkers preparing for a long day in the fields. Due to this fact, the first meal of the day is often also the heaviest. Typical dishes include *queso frito* (deep-fried cheese), *huevos revueltos* (scrambled eggs served with or without bits of ham), *mangú* (mashed plantains mixed with oil and fried onion), fresh orange juice, and lashings of coffee *con leche* (with milk) sweetened with plenty of sugar.

Lunch

Lunch is enjoyed during the traditional two-hour break at midday. Chicken is almost always served in some form in addition to mouth-watering treats like *bistec encebollado* (grilled steak with onions and peppers), *mofongo* (a melange of garlic, plantains and pork rinds), and *mondongo* (tripe stew). On special occasions, *cassava* (Taino crispy flatbread made with Yucca roots), *chivo* (roast goat) or *sancocho* (a stew made with five different kinds of meat, four different types of tuber, plenty of vegetables and numerous spices) may also be dished up. Festivals are always a good time to sample these delicacies.

Dinner

Always a big family affair, dinner is the one meal when Dominicans can expect every brother, cousin, sister and aunt to come home from a day at work, play or

Catch of the day

Cool and colourful: the perfect sundowner

Coffee beans ripen in the sun

school. Unlike in North America or Europe, restaurants are reserved for special occasions only – and they are never eaten at alone. Chicken is the usual main course, so it is the days when seafood is offered that are truly special. Dominicans traditionally prepare seafood in one of five deliciously different ways: *al horno* (roasted with lemon), *al ajillo* (served in a garlic sauce), *al oregano* (prepared in a heavy cream and oregano sauce), *criolla* (spicy tomato sauce) or *con coco* (a blend of garlic, tomato and coconut milk). The best fish and seafood to choose from include *langosta* (clawless lobster), *pulpo* (octopus), *mero* (sea bass), *carite* (kingfish), *cangrejo* (crab), *chillo* (red snapper), *lambí* (conch) – and absolutely stunning *camarones* (shrimp).

You can pretty much bet that any fish or seafood you eat at dinner was happily swimming around in the Caribbean earlier the same day.

Dessert

Dominican desserts are extremely sweet. Cakes, custards and flans are ever popular, especially a particular local type of corn-based custard known as *flan de maiz*. Other local delicacies include *dulces de naranja* (molasses and orange marmalade), *dulces con coco* (molasses and coconut shavings), and *dulces con leche* (a molasses and sweet milk blend). Those watching their weight may prefer the Dominican's dizzying array of fresh tropical fruit. Bananas, pineapples, strawberries, mangoes and papayas are all grown on the island. For a new taste sensation, try *chinola* (a native passion fruit) and *limoncillos* (lime-like fruit sold in bunches).

What to drink
Alcoholic drinks

There are plenty of brands of beer to enjoy while you slowly sizzle in the sun. The most popular label of the bunch is Presidente. Bottles of Presidente are usually larger than you might be used to, so be sure to work up a thirst before you order one.

Rum is another speciality of the island; specifically Brugal, Barceló and Bermúdez. If you ask a local, they will probably tell you that Bermúdez is the best of the bunch, but the dark, aged versions of the other brands are not bad either.

If you want your rum to last the evening, order a *Cuba libre servicio* at any disco or bar and you will get a bottle of rum, two Cokes and a big bucket of ice. Always check to make sure the ice was not frozen from the local tap water before you enjoy. If you are normally a wine drinker, you may want to rethink your habit for the duration of this holiday. Dominican wine is not of the highest quality and imported wine is expensive. One local drink that is made with wine is *Mama Juana*. Local wine, honey, rum, tree bark and leaves go into this potent combination, which is buried underground for three weeks and then laid out in the sun for another three. It is very much an acquired taste,

but it reputedly prolongs sexual potency and lifespan.

Non-alcoholic drinks
If you don't drink, or if you are just looking for something non-alcoholic to imbibe while you sit in the sun, then you are in luck: the Dominican Republic offers plenty of tasty non-alcoholic options for you to enjoy. Fresh coconut milk is drunk by almost everyone, and is available from the vendors lining every street on the island. Fruit shakes are also extremely popular; these are made from ice, milk and any of the native fruits grown in the Dominican, including

A stunning seafood platter

Fresh coconut? Coming right up

Harvest time in the sugar-cane fields

papaya, banana, pineapple and the perennial favourite, mango. For something even sweeter, give your fruit shake a Dominican twist. *Morir soñando* is a concoction of sugar, condensed milk, orange juice and crushed ice, and is drunk in almost every home in the nation.

But it is at breakfast that the Dominican Republic truly shines. Fresh orange juice is a Dominican breakfast staple. From tree to tasting can take as little as five minutes if you are in the countryside near the groves where they are grown. If you don't have a sweet tooth, ask for it *sin azúcar* (without sugar).

Dominican coffee is a taste of heaven and is considered among the best in the world. Most of the best beans are grown in the Cordillera Central mountain range. Coffee can be purchased almost anywhere in the country from street vendors. Locals traditionally take it *solo* (black with plenty of sugar). *Café con leche* is made with steamed milk and tastes divine. The best place to get a good cup is a *comedor*. Expect to pay about RD$5–10.

Meal prices

Prices at Dominican restaurants vary wildly, according to whether you are eating at a family-run local café or an 'international' dining establishment. Prices in this guide are subject to fluctuation and should only be used as a rough guide.

   * under US$10
   ** US$10–$20
   *** US$20–$30
   **** over US$30

Guide prices are per person for a main course at dinner, excluding drinks.

WHERE TO EAT
Barahona restaurants
Brisas del Caribe**

Open-air restaurant with beautiful views of the Caribbean. Seafood – especially lobster and shrimp – are the speciality of the house. *Avenida Enriquillo 1. Tel: (809) 524 2794.*

D'Lina Pizza*

Large – and good – pizzas that should sate your appetite for several hours. *Corner of Avenida 30 de Mayo and Calle Anacaona. No telephone.*

La Rocca*

Open-air, but lacking a beachside perspective. Good food makes up for the lack of a view. Menu covers all the meat and seafood bases. *Avenida Enriquillo 14. No telephone.*

Boca Chica restaurants
Deli-Beach*

Need a dependable beach-side lunch but don't want to fork out a fortune? Grab yourself a burger or sandwich at this beachside eatery and enjoy. *East end of Avenida Duarte. No telephone.*

El Pelicano**

Amazing seafood that is

Locals enjoy friendly service at an open-air café

so fresh you could swear it's still swimming. The red snapper and spiny lobsters are especially tasty. *Coral Hamaca Beach Hotel. Tel: (809) 523 6505.*

Restaurant Boca Marina***

Seafood specialities served in a delightful open-air eatery. Sit at the wooden tables under the covered deck as you lap up the pleasant sea breezes. The food isn't bad either. *Calle Duarte 12. Tel: (809) 523 6702.*

Cabarete
Café Pitu*

Casual café that does amazing things with anything green. The Greek salad is especially delicious. *East side of town on the beach. No telephone.*

Panadería Repostería Dick y Café House*

Famous for its breakfasts featuring the best freshly squeezed orange juice you will ever taste. It's like drinking a ray of sunshine.

West side of town on the main street. Tel: (809) 571 0612.

Restaurant at Natura Cabanas**

While all meals at this al-fresco *boite* are notable, breakfast should be your reason to book. Listen to the waves break on the coral rock and take in the sight of early morning horse riders on the beach.

Natura Cabanas, Perla Marina. Tel: (809) 571 1507.

Constanza

Lorenzo's Restaurant Café*

Basic food that will serve you well in a town not exactly brimming with culinary possibilities. Play it safe and order either the guinea fowl or wild rabbit, their two best dishes.

Luperón 83. No telephone.

La Montaña*

Simple breakfasts and local favourites in a pleasant atmosphere. Not quite as good as Lorenzo's but a good alternative.

Ureña 40. No telephone.

Jarabacoa

Del Parque Galeria Restaurant*

Jarabacoa's weekend hotspot is a great place to enjoy a drink and tasty finger-foods. Go for the people-watching more than for the food. Snagging a table on Saturday and Sunday afternoons can be tricky.

Corner of Duarte and Mirabal. No telephone.

D'Parrillada Restaurant**

The best food in Jarabacoa, especially if you like fine cuts of steak.

A selection of sweets to savour

Bottles of rum on the factory conveyor belt

Vegetarians should stay well clear.
Avenida Independencía 1. No telephone. Closed Mon.
Restaurante El Rancho**
The fanciest restaurant in town – El Rancho is where moneyed locals go. International cuisine is well prepared. Artwork by local artists can be purchased right off the walls.
Corner of Avenida Independencía and Avenida Norberto Tiburcio. No telephone.

La Romana
Don Quijote**
Delicious seafood, steaks and international cuisine are the order of the day at this great dining spot boasting one of the finest chefs in town.
Calle Diego Avila 44. Tel: (809) 556 2827.
El Patio**
Nouvelle Dominican cuisine given a splash of something extra. Traditional dishes are flawless and well worth trying. Everything is lovingly prepared. It's a

gourmet salute to national pride.
Casa de Campo. Tel: (809) 523 8548.
Shish Kebab Restaurant*
Middle Eastern specialities that taste great. *Baba ghanoush,* stuffed grape leaves and – of course – shish kebab are all tastily available.
Calle Francisco del Castillo Marquéz 32. Tel: (809) 556 2737.

Lago Enriquillo
Brahaman's*
The only restaurant with palatable food in La Descubierta. Prepare to go more to fill your stomach than for any memorable taste sensations.
Deligne 1. No telephone.

Playa Dorada
Hemingway's Café**
Hemingway-themed eatery that's high on kitsch. '*For Whom the Bell Tolls*' fajitas anyone? A fun place to mix with a young crowd. It can get noisy.
Playa Dorada Plaza. Tel: (809) 320 2230.

Puerto Plata
Acuarela***
Fusion Dominican cuisine served in a

120-year-old home surrounded by beautiful gardens. Much loved by rich ex-pats and moneyed locals.

Polanca Bar-Restaurante**

Unassuming eatery that serves delicious seafood. Don't let the tatty interior dissuade you from going in.

Calle John F Kennedy 25. Tel: (809) 586 9174. Closed Sunday.

El Provocón*

Grilled chicken like you have never tasted before. A whole chicken will only set you back a few dollars!

Peeling plantains for hungry customers

Calle Separación 19. Tel: (809) 970 1200.

Punta Cana
La Yola***

Open-air seafood restaurant located right on the water. The dishes are simple and delicious – no fancy sauces or rich creams here. All entrées are served with yummy yucca fries.

La Marina, Punta Cana Resort & Club. Tel: (809) 221 2262, ext. 7124.

Samaná
Café de Paris*

Salads, pizzas and pancakes to assuage those mid-afternoon hunger pangs.

Avenida la Marina. No telephone.

Restaurant Camilo*

Sip a cocktail and dig into the menu of Dominican staples. The view overlooking the bay should be enough to satisfy even the most demanding patron.

Avenida la Marina. Tel: (809) 538 2781.

Villa Serena**

Fresh fish served on the beach. Desserts are homemade and worth saving room for.

Villa Serena Hotel. Tel: (809) 696 0065.

San Pedro de Macoris
Apolo**
It lacks a bit in terms of the interior décor, but this place serves the best steaks in town.
Independencía 53. Tel: (809) 529-3549.

Santiago
Cafeteria del Sol*
Budget-conscious Dominican food in a cafeteria-style eatery that caters to locals.
Corner of Calle del Sol and Calle 30 de Marzo. No telephone.
Kukara Makara**
Howdy pardner! Sit on down at this tex-mex restaurant for some hardy chow. The theme is a bit overdone but you will soon be yelling 'yee-haw' over your plate of fajitas.
Corner of Avenida Francia and Calle del Sol. Tel: (809) 241 3143.
Restaurante El Pabellón*
A slice of Chinatown in the heart of the Caribbean. Although the dishes will not exactly transport you to Shanghai, the egg rolls will give you something of the flavour of the Orient.
Calle del Sol 23. Tel: (809) 581 5772.

Santo Domingo
La Briciola****
If you insist on eating Italian food while you're in the capital, then this is your best bet. The *osso buco* is absolutely amazing.
Calle Arzobispo Merino 152-A. Tel: (809) 688 5055. Jacket required. Closed Sun.
Caribbean Blue***
Contemporary dining in a chic, restored 16th-century building. If nouvelle cuisine is your thing, then the main courses – in the form of delicate shrimp paired with rocket, or papaya with tamarind vinaigrette – are sure to tantalise the tastebuds.
Calle Hostos 205. Tel: (809) 682 1238. Closed Sun.
El Conuco**
A beautiful eatery that resembles a hidden jungle in the heart of the capital city. Dominican dishes are the speciality of this popular dining spot, and the lush location also makes it extremely romantic.
Calle Casimiro de Moya 152. Tel: (809) 686 0129.
El Meson de la Cava***
Contemporary continental cuisine served in a fascinating setting: a real cave that once housed runaway pirates. While the food can be a bit uninspiring, the location and atmosphere more than make up for the menu's lack of originality.
1 Avenida Mirador del Sur. Tel: (809) 532 2615.
Paco Cafetería*
Daily specials enjoyed by locals. You'll probably be the only gringo in the place.
Corner of El Conde and Palo Hincado. No telephone.
Scherezade***
A touch of Marrakech in the heart of the Caribbean. Waiters wear fez hats, Moorish tiles surround and hummus is produced by the gallon. Occasional evenings feature flamenco dancers.
Avenida Roberto Pastoriza 226. Tel: (809) 227 2323. Closed Mon.

Sosúa
Johnnie's*
Widely acknowledged to serve the best chicken sandwiches in town. Wildly popular – but the reputation is justly deserved.
Calle Arzeno near Calle Pedro Clisante. No telephone.

La Puntilla de Piergiorgio**
This gorgeous eatery is situated on the top of a seaside cliff and is surrounded by bougainvillea. While the Italian food on the menu is not much more than passable, a seat here at sunset will make your meal truly memorable.
Piergiorgio Palace Hotel, Calle La Puntilla 1. Tel: (809) 571 2215.

Restaurant Pollo Rico**
Swiss-owned restaurant that will take you right back to the continent. While the menu is varied, the German dishes are the best.
Calle Pedro Clisante 14. Tel: (809) 571 3322.

Rich pickings: these bananas will soon be ready for harvesting

Hotels and Accommodation

There is no official star classification system operated by the Dominican Republic Tourist Board. However, there are plenty of properties scattered throughout the country that cater to all budgets and styles. The Dominican Republic boasts over 55,000 hotel rooms – more than any other country in the Caribbean. Room rates in Santo Domingo are generally the same year-round. Beach resorts, however, have high winter and discounted summer rates. August can see room rates drop by as much as 50 per cent.

Bellhop at the Renaissance Jaragua Hotel and Casino

The country is well known for its all-inclusive possibilities, especially in the resort areas along the north coast. For small inns and pensiones, however, your best bet is to look in Sosúa and Cabarete. However, all-inclusive mega-resorts do exist here in both towns, so be sure to double-check the style of your property before making any assumptions.

If you haven't made a booking before arriving in the country, information on accommodation can be obtained from Tourist Information at Santo Domingo International Airport. There is also an information office on the Malecón in Puerto Plata.

Santo Domingo

From five-star resorts to dorm-style places, there are plenty of options for accommodation in the Dominican Republic's capital city. The bulk of the luxury hotels in Santo Domingo can be found straddling the Malecón. Expect to pay in the region of £50–75 per night for a double room.

If you are looking for culture and history, then a room in a restored, historic, three-star property in the Zona Colonial should cost you in the region of £40 per night. Budget properties in the city vary wildly in terms of quality. Always check your room before you hand over any money. Rooms can be had for as little as £10 per night.

Luxury Hotels

Barceló Gran Hotel Lina *Avenida Máximo Gómez. Tel: (809) 563 5000. www.barcelo-hotels.com*
Centenario Inter-Continental *Malecón 218. Tel: (809) 221 1889. www.santo-domingo.interconti.com*
Hotel Santo Domingo *Avenidas Independencia and Abraham Lincoln. Tel: (809) 221 1511. www.hotel.stodgo.com.do.*
Meliá Santo Domingo Hotel and Casino *Avenida George Washington 365. Tel: (809) 221 6666. www.solmelia.es*
Occidental El Embajador and Casino *Avenida Sarasota 65. Tel: (809) 221 2131.*

www.occidental-hoteles.com
Renaissance Jaragua Hotel and Casino
Avenida George Washington 367. Tel:
(809) 221 2222.
www.renaissancehotels.com

Boutique and mid-priced hotels
Caribe Colonial *Isabela 159. Tel: (809)*
688 7799. www.hodelpa.com
El Napolitano *Malecón 101. Tel: (809)*
687 1131. www.hotelnapolitano.com
Hotel Sofitel Francés *Mercedes and Arz*
Meriño. Tel: (809) 685 9331.
www.sofitel.com
Nicolás Nader *Luperón 151. Tel: (809)*
687 6674.
Palacio *Duarte 106. Tel: (809) 682 4730.*

www.hotelpalacio.com
Plaza Colonial *Pellerano and Jules Verne.*
Tel: (809) 687 9111.

Budget hotels
Anacona *Calle Isidro Pérez and*
Hincando. Tel: (809) 688 6888.
Bettye's Guest House *Isabela 163. Tel:*
(809) 688 7649.
Felicidad *Aristides Cabrar 58. Tel: (809)*
221 6615.
Ginette *El Conde 505. Tel: (809) 685*
7815.
Hostal Hostos *Hostos 299. Tel: (809) 688*
9192.
La Grand Mansión *Danae 26. Tel: (809)*
689 8758.

Hotel courtyards provide welcome shade

A tranquil salon at the Melía Caribe Tropical, Bávaro

The rest of the country

With no official star-rating system in the Dominican Republic, any rankings are subjective. As such, the properties listed outside of Santo Domingo have been rated according to price.

*	under US$25 per night
**	US$25–$75 per night
***	US$75–$100 per night
****	over US$100 per night

Barahona
Barceló Bahoruco Beach Resort* *Carretera del la Costa, Km 17. Tel: (809) 524 1111. www.barcelo-hotels.com*
Cacique* *Avenida Uruguay 2. Tel: (809) 524 4620.*
Caribe* *Avenida Enriquillo 14. Tel: (809) 524 4111.*
Casa Bonita* *Barahona. Tel: (809) 696 0215.*

Gran Hotel Barahona* *Calle Jaime Mota 5. Tel: (809) 524 3442.*
San Martin* *Calle Duarte 6. Tel: (809) 524 5821.*

Bávaro
Bávaro Beach Resort* *Bávaro. Tel: (809) 686 5797. www.barcelo.com*
Meliá Caribe Tropical** *Bávaro. Tel: (809) 221 2311 www.solmelia.es.*
Natura Park* *Bávaro. Tel: (809) 538 3111.*

Boca Chica
Barceló Capella Beach Resort* *Juan Dolio. Tel: (809) 526 1080. www.barcelo-hotels.com*
Boca Chica Beach Resort* *Vicini and 20 de Diciembre. Tel: (809) 523 4521.*
Casa Coco* *Dominguez 8. Tel: (809) 523 4409.*

Coral Hamaca Beach Hotel and Casino*** *Avenida Hamaca Beach Resort. Tel: (809) 523 4611. www.coralhotels.com.do.*
Europa** *Dominguez and Duarte. Tel: (809) 523 5721.*
Romagna Mia* *Duarte 1. Tel: (809) 523 4647.*

Cabarete
Banana Boat* *Carretera 5. Tel: (809) 571 0690.*
Cabarete Beach Hotel**** *Playa Cabarete. Tel: (809) 571 0755.*

Casa del Surf* *Carretera 5. Tel: (809) 571 0736.*
Hotel Sans Souci** *Playa Cabarete. Tel: (809) 571 0755.*
Natura Cabanas*** *Playa Perla Marina. Tel: (809) 571 1507. www.naturacabana.com*
Palm Beach Condos**** *Carretera 5. Tel: (809) 571 0758. www.cabaretecondos.com*
Sea Horse Ranch**** *Cabarete. Tel: (809) 571 3880. www.sea-horse-ranch.com*
Tropical Beach Club Hotel** *Playa Cabarete. Tel: (809) 571 0956. www.tropicalclubs.com*
Windsurf Hotel*** *Carretera Principal. Tel: (809) 571 0718. www.sunsetresorts.com*

Constanza
Altocerro* *Colonia Kennedy. Tel: (809) 530 6192.*
Cabañas de las Montaña** *Colonia Kennedy. Tel: (809) 539 3268.*
Hotel Restaurant Mi Casa* *Corner of Luperón and Sanchez. Tel: (809) 539 2764.*

Jarabacoa
Giselle* *Carretera Jarabacoa Km 10. Tel: (809) 574 4433.*
Gran Jimenoa** *Avenida La Confluencia, Los Corralitos. Tel: (809) 574 6304.*
Hogar* *Mella 34. Tel: (809) 574 2739.*
Jarabacoa River Resort** *La Confluencia. Tel: (809) 574 4688.*

The casino at Playa Dorada Hotel

The Dominican Republic has accommodation to suit all tastes

Rancho Baiguate*** *Road to Constanza 5km (3 miles). Tel: (809) 574 6890.*

La Isabela/El Castillo
Miramar** *Calle Vista del Mar, El Castillo. Tel: (809) 471 9157.*
Rancho del Sol* *Carretera de las Américas, El Castillo. Tel: (809) 543 8172.*

La Romana
Casa de Campo**** *La Romana (Box 140). Tel: (809) 523 3333. www.casadecampo.com*
Casa del Mar*** *Bayahibe Bay, La Romana. Tel: (809) 221 8880. www.AMHSAmarina.com*

Frano** *Avenida Padre Abreu 9. Tel: (809) 550 4744.*

Lago Enriquillo
Hotel del Lago* *Corner of Mella and Billini, La Descubierta. Tel: (809) 224 9525.*
Hotel Jimaní* *On the road going east out of Jimaní. Tel: (809) 248 3139.*
Padre Billini* *Billini 26, La Descubierta. Tel: (809) 696 0327.*

Playa Dorada
Caribbean Village Club on the Green**** *Playa Dorada. Tel: (809) 320 1111. www.allegroresorts.com*

Flamenco Beach Resort★★★★ *Playa Dorada. Tel: (809) 320 5084. www.occidental-hoteles.com*
Playa Dorada Hotel & Casino★★★★ *Playa Dorada. Tel: (809) 320 3988. www.occidental-hoteles.com*
Playa Naco Golf & Tennis Resort★★★ *Playa Dorada. Tel: (809) 320 4003. www.naco.com.do.*
Victoria Resort★★★★ *Playa Dorada. Tel: (809) 320 1200. www.victoriahoteles.com.do.*

Puerto Plata
Atlantic Guest House★ *Calle 12 de Julio 24. Tel: (809) 586 2503.*

Hotel Ilra★ *Calle Villa Nueva 25. Tel: (809) 586 2337.*
Hotel Latin Quarter★ *Avenida Circunvalación Norte 90. Tel: (809) 586 2588.*
Puerto Plata Beach Resort & Casino★★★★ *Avenida Circunvalación Norte 89. Tel: (809) 586 4243.*
Sofy's Bed and Breakfast★★ *Las Rosas 3. Tel: (809) 586 6411.*
Swedish Guest House★ *Avenida Circunvalación Sur 157. Tel: (809) 586 5086.*

Punta Cana
Club Med Punta Cana★★★ *Punta Cana.*

A comfortable room with a view

Service comes with a smile

Tel: (809) 687 2767.
Meliá Caribe Tropical**** *Punta Cana. Tel: (809) 221 1290. www.solmelia.es.*
Punta Cana Beach Resort** *Playa Punta Cana. Tel: (809) 221 2262. www.puntacana.com*

Samaná
Bahia View* *Avenida Circunvalación. Tel: (809) 538 2186.*
Cayacoa Resort** *Calle Cayacoa. Tel: (809) 538 3111.*
Cotubanama* *Avenida Rosario Sánchez and Santa Bárbara. Tel: (809) 538 2557.*

Occidental Gran Bahia** *Las Cacao. Tel: (809) 538 3111. www.occidental-hoteles.com*
Playa Colibri*** *Avenida de la Mar, Las Terrenas. Tel: (809) 240 6434. www.playacolibri.com*
Villa Serena*** *Las Galeras. Tel: (809) 538 0000.*

San Pedro de Macoris
Howard Johnson Hotel Macorix** *Malecón. Tel: (809) 529 2100.*
Pensión Sandy* *Carretera 3 and Deligne. No telephone.*
Río Vista* *Malecón 1. Tel: (809) 529 7555.*

Santiago

Centro Plaza** *Mella 54. Tel: (809) 581 7000.*

Hostal Aloha Sol*** *Calle del Sol 150. Tel: (809) 583 0090.*

Hostal del Cibao* *Calle Benito Monción 40. Tel: (809) 581 7775.*

Hostal Don José* *Calle Colón 42. Tel: (809) 581 7480.*

Hostal Matún** *Las Carreras 1. Tel: (809) 581 3107.*

Sosúa

Apart-Hotel Europa Sosúa** *Calle Pedro Clisante 13. Tel: (809) 571 3335.*

Casa Marina Beach**** *Calle Dr Alejo Martínez. Tel: (809) 571 3690. www.amshamarina.com*

Hotel Garden Keti* *Calle Dr Rosen 32. Tel: (809) 571 1557. www.hotelgardenketi.com*

Hotel Sosúa** *Calle Duarte. Tel: (809) 571 2683.*

On the Waterfront* *Calle Dr Rosen 1. Tel: (809) 571 2670. www.hotelwaterfront.com*

PierGiorgio Palace Hotel*** *Calle La Puntilla. Tel: (809) 571 2215. www.piergiorgiohotel.com*

Playa Enscondida Beach Resort*** *Calle AP Chiquita. Tel: (809) 471 5040. www.amhsamarina.com*

Left luggage: the Dominican is the Caribbean's most popular destination

On Business

The Dominican Republic is one of the poorest countries in the Western Hemisphere. The government is doing its best to entice investment in both the tourism and manufacturing industries. Since its boom in the 1980s, the tourism industry has brought about a lot of changes that benefit residents and visitors alike: major highways have been resurfaced; pavements, lighting and signage in urban areas are much improved, rubbish pick-up is more frequent, and security – especially the security of visiting nationals – is considered paramount.

Heading for work in the nation's capital

Dominican business and business practices are heavily influenced by America. Even the streets in the capital city are named after American presidents. Many locals speak basic English, especially in the major tourist locations.

Business hours

Most businesses open 8.30am to 12.30pm and 2.30pm to 6.30pm, Monday to Friday. Shops, restaurants and other businesses serving the tourist industry usually open on Saturday as well. Banks open from 8am to 4pm Monday to Friday. Government office hours are officially 7.30am to 2.30pm. However, it is an unwritten rule that only secretaries arrive before 9am, so if you need anything 'official' done for you, there's no point going too early.

A lunchtime siesta of approximately two hours is common practice for all businesses. When you experience the power of the Caribbean sun at midday, you'll understand why.

Dress

The Dominicans rate personal appearance very highly. When going for a meeting or for an evening of drinks and dinner, women should wear long skirts and men trousers and shirtsleeves, even during the hottest days of the year. Trousers and long skirts are particularly vital if you are thinking of visiting a holy site. Men wearing shorts or women wearing skirts above the knee will not be allowed inside any church.

Never wear shorts outside of your hotel if you do not want to stand out as a typical tourist. And those who sport an uncombed, unshaven appearance will be positively frowned upon, no matter how 'designer chic' the look may be back home. When in doubt, shave.

Tipping

If you are entertaining clients, then you will need to know how to tip the staff. Most Dominican restaurants add a 10 per cent service charge to their bills. However, all locals know that this charge is rarely actually given to the waiters or waitresses, and so they give an additional 10 per cent directly to the waiting staff to compensate. This is something that you should do too if you don't want to look cheap.

The Internet

If you are coming to the Dominican Republic for a short period, don't bring your laptop. Local services are slow and unreliable. It usually takes two weeks to set up an account. Fluctuations in the local power supply can also fry your hard drive.

A better option is to use an Internet café. Typical rates range between RD$25 and RD$50 per hour. Always make sure the café has a minimum DSL connection.

Hotels are just beginning to introduce Internet services in rooms, but coverage is still sketchy at best. Free Internet services are often available at high-end resorts, but these are often limited to a maximum of 20 minutes' usage time.

Driving ambition – reaping the benefits of a well-paid job

Practical Guide

ARRIVING
Formalities

Visitors coming to the Dominican
Republic who are citizens of the UK,
Ireland, Australia, the US, Canada, and
all other EU countries will need a
passport, but not a visa for stays up to
90 days. New Zealanders will require a
60-day visa for the Dominican Republic
issued by the consulate in Australia at a
cost of A$80.

All visitors to the Dominican
Republic require a tourist card issued at
the airport or cruise terminal upon
arrival for around £5. All nationalities
will be required to show a return ticket
home before entering the Dominican
Republic. US and Canadian citizens
can substitute a birth certificate and
government-issued photo ID for
the passport.

Arriving by air

Many major schedules airlines serve the
Dominican Republic including Air
Canada, Air France, Iberia, Continental,
American, Delta, USAir and Northwest.
Numerous charter airlines also fly to the

A Dominican Republic entry visa

country. There are no scheduled non-
stop services from the UK, Ireland,
Australia or New Zealand.

There are seven international airports
serving the country, but the majority of
them only fly in charter planes. There
are three airports that land scheduled
services.

Aeropuerto Internacional Las
Américas (Tel: 549 0858/0002) is the
largest airport in the country, which
serves the capital city of Santo Domingo
and is located 13km (8 miles) east of the
city. Aeropuerto Internacional Gregorio
Luperón (Tel: 586 0129) is the main
gateway for travellers staying in Puerto
Plata, Sosúa and the mega resort of
Playa Dorada.

Aeropuerto Internacional Cibao
(Tel: 226 0664) serves Santiago and the
Cibao region.

Arriving by sea

Three major cruise lines visit the
Dominican Republic: Holland America,
Carnival and Norwegian. In each case,
Puerto Plata and/or Santo Domingo are
the only Dominican ports of call on
their varied itineraries.

Cars and driving
Breakdown

The Dominican Republic is not an easy
country in which to have car trouble. If
you do have a problem, your only
option is to get your car or motorcycle
to the nearest repair shop somehow, and
apply for a loan to pay off the exorbitant
fees you will be charged.

Car hire

Rental prices are extremely expensive in the Dominican Republic, averaging out at about £25 per day – and that is not including the optional insurance that will set you back a further £5–6 per day.

A credit card will be required for your deposit. Without one you will be prey to no-name firms that specialise in renting cars at sky-high rates. Always note every scratch, dent or problem before you drive away from the hire company's car park. Even if you get collision insurance, Dominican law states that you are liable for all damage to the vehicle up to a value of RD$25,000.

Taxi, please

Driving

Traffic police are probably the biggest bar to enjoyable driving in the Dominican Republic. Famous for their corrupt ways, they will pull you over for even the most minor of violations in the hope of extracting a bribe. One good trick is to keep a small amount of money in your wallet and the bulk of your funds hidden somewhere else. When you pull out your wallet to pay the 'fee', the officer will see that you've emptied your wallet and will, with any luck, send you on your way.

Dominican drivers may honk if they feel you are going too slowly for their comfort, but they will eventually pass you if you give them the opportunity.

Potholes are all too common and often large enough to cause serious damage to your vehicle.

Fuel

A gallon of fuel will cost in the region of RD$40. Be sure to keep your tank half full at all times. Petrol stations close by 7pm and often run out of supplies.

Traffic regulations

In the Dominican Republic, driving is on the right-hand side. Always give way to buses and cargo trucks on the major highways; they will constantly attempt to overtake you anyway. As you approach major towns and cities, keep an eye out for speed bumps. They were originally put in place to lower the number of accidents, but are now often used by the traffic police to slow cars down so that they can collect a RD$5 'toll' from the driver.

Crime and police

Crime against tourists is generally limited to petty theft and pickpocketing. Should you find yourself victim to a mugging, do not argue or fight back. Give the mugger what they ask for. Keep all valuables like expensive watches or jewellery in the hotel; never wear them outside. When leaving valuables in your hotel room, always use the hotel safe. Staff are paid extremely low wages and have been known to 'borrow' a thing or two – especially passports. Carry a fake wallet or purse on you with a small amount of cash. If you are pick-pocketed or attacked, you will have a greater chance of getting away with less of a loss.

If you find yourself in the middle of a demonstration, get out immediately. The local police usually respond to unauthorized demonstrations with bullets and beatings.

Custom regulations

Duty free is available to all who visit the Dominican Republic from outside the country without incurring import taxes. Visitors are permitted to bring in up to one litre of alcohol, 200 cigarettes and gifts not exceeding a value of about £50.

CROSSING BETWEEN THE DOMINICAN REPUBLIC AND HAITI

If you have plans to cross into Haiti, do not rent a car to do it. You will not be covered by the insurance that you take out with a Dominican rental agency. Even if you were permitted to cross the border, car theft rates in Haiti should be enough to convince you that it is not a wise idea. The easiest way to enter Haiti is to cross with one of the two Dominican companies that make the trip – Terrabus and Caribe Tours. Do not forget your tourist card whenever you move between the countries.

Electricity

The standard electrical current is 115 to 125 volts AC, 60 Hz with two and three-pin plugs. This is the same system as the US and Canada. Appliances from these countries can be used safely. Electrical

A busy bus ride

Keeping the peace

appliances from other countries will require an adaptor. Power outages are common. Always check with the hotel you are staying in whether or not they have an on-site generator.

Embassies and consulates

As the capital of the country, Santo Domingo is where you will need to go if you require assistance from your embassy. Please note that Ireland, Australia and New Zealand have no consular representation in the Dominican Republic. Should visitors from these countries require diplomatic assistance, they should contact the UK embassy.

American Embassy, Av César Nicolás Penson. Tel: (809) 221 2171.
British Embassy, Av 27 de Febrero 233. Tel: (809) 472 7111.
Canadian Embassy, Av Eugenio de Marchena 39. Tel: (809) 685 1136.

Emergency numbers

In the event that you find yourself in an emergency situation, dial 911. The police will respond rapidly if you are a tourist.

Health

The major health risks during your stay

The Dominican flag

will be eating contaminated food, drinking contaminated water, exposure to the sun and mosquito bites. Be sure to drink only bottled water and eat only fruit that you can peel. If you have any doubts at all about an item, do not eat or drink it. Check the seal of your water bottle to make sure that it has not been tampered with or refilled with tap water.

No special inoculations are required for a visit to the Dominican Republic, but it is a good idea to keep up to date with your tetanus and polio vaccinations. Hepatitis A and B inoculations are also strongly recommended. You should not require any malaria medication, unless you are travelling near the Haitian border or in the Parque Nacional Los Haitises.

The Dominican Republic has epidemic-level transmission rates of HIV/AIDS. Always use a condom if you have sex while abroad, and do bring condoms with you: condoms in the Dominican Republic are not of the same quality that you would find at home. It is a good idea to take your own syringes or needles, but if you do not have them and require an injection of any sort, insist on a new needle.

Insurance

You should take out personal travel insurance from your travel agent, tour operator or insurance company. It should give adequate coverage for medical expenses, loss or theft, repatriation, personal liability, third-party motor insurance (but liability arising from accidents is not usually included) and cancellation expenses. Always read the conditions and check that the amount of coverage is adequate.

LANGUAGE

The official language of the Dominican Republic is Spanish. If you plan on sticking to the major resorts, you should be fine with English, but elsewhere you will find that Spanish is the only language understood. Although in some respects it is a more complicated language than English, in one respect it is easier: words are pronounced as they look, according to a few simple rules.

PRONUNCIATION

Generally the accent falls on the second-to-last syllable unless it is marked with a written accent.

Vowel Sounds

Vowels are always pronounced in the same way:

a ah   **o** oh

e eh   **u** oo

i ee

Consonant Sounds

Consonants are the same as in English with the following exceptions:

ll like 'y' in 'yes'

rr is strongly trilled in a way that does not exist in English

h is silent

j like a guttural 'h'

g followed by 'e' or 'i' like a guttural 'h'

ñ Like 'nio' as in 'onion'

USEFUL WORDS AND PHRASES

yes	si
no	no
please	por favor
thank you	gracias
you are welcome	de nada
bon appetit	buen provecho
hello	hola
goodbye	adiós
morning	mañana
good morning	buenos días
afternoon/evening	tarde
good afternoon/ good evening	buenas tardes
night	noche
good night	buenas noches
cheap	barato
expensive	caro
near	cerca
far	lejos
day	día
week	semana
month	mes
year	año

NUMBERS

1	uno
2	dos
3	tres
4	cuatro
5	cinco
6	seis
7	siete
8	ocho
9	nueve
10	diez

DAYS OF THE WEEK

Sunday	domingo
Monday	lunes
Tuesday	martes
Wednesday	miércoles
Thursday	jueves
Friday	viernes
Saturday	sábado

Media

There are no English-language news publications in the Dominican Republic. If you read Spanish, you can keep up with current events with either the quality *Listin Diario* or the more tabloid-style *El Siglo*.

Dominican radio is flooded with Latin music, with the occasional American/European pop station thrown in the mix. Cable television features over 80 stations, half of which are English-language.

MONEY MATTERS

The currency in the Dominican Republic is the peso (RD$). US dollars are also widely accepted, especially in the high-end resorts. The currency denominations are: 5, 10, 20, 50, 100, 500, 1,000 and 5,000 peso notes and 0.10, 0.25, 0.50 and 1 peso coins. You can take out money from your account or on your credit card at many Dominican ATM machines. However, ATM machines are usually restricted to major cities and resort towns.

Changing money

If you are staying at an all-inclusive resort, change your money at the airport when you arrive, as the resorts offer terrible exchange rates. All other travellers should change their money at local banks when possible.

Credit cards

Credit cards are valid at almost all mid-range and pricey establishments in the cities and resort towns, but less so in rural areas. Visa is the most widely accepted and convenient of the brands;

Check duty-free limits before stocking up

Mastercard and American Express are also useful, however.

Pharmacies

If you need any medications while abroad, bring them from home. If you run out of your prescription, you will have to go to a private clinic: the costs will be much higher than you are used to.

Postal services

If you want your postcards to arrive at their destination in the same month that you post them, you will have to send them special delivery – and that still does not guarantee anything. Postage costs RD$3 to North America and RD$4 for everywhere else.

Public holidays

The Dominican Republic's public holidays are:

January 1 New Year's Day
January 6 Epiphany/Three Kings Day
January 21 Our Lady of Altagracia
January 26 Duarte Day
February 27 Independence Day

March/April Holy Thursday, Holy Friday, Easter Sunday
April 14 Pan-American Day
May 1 Labour Day
July 16 Foundation of Sociedad la Trinitaria
August 16 Restoration Day
September 24 Our Lady of Mercedes
October 12 Columbus Day
October 24 United Nations Day
November 1 All Saints' Day
December 25 Christmas Day

Public transport
Buses
Buses are an effective way both of covering long distances and seeing the country. Metro Bus and Caribe Tours offer affordable, comfortable, air-conditioned rides to most of the country's major destinations.

Gua-Guas
Similar to Metro Bus and Caribe Tours coaches, *gua-guas* are less comfortable than their more luxurious cousins. For short distances (e.g. Puerto Plata to Playa Dorada), they're a cheap and easy way of getting from one point to another.

The Dominican Republic peso in coins and notes

Religious worship
The vast majority of Dominicans (98 per cent) are Roman Catholic. However, few are what one would consider devout. The north coast town of Sosúa once boasted a large population of Jews. Most of them have left the country, but evidence of their occupation remains in the form of a synagogue and Jewish history museum.

Taxis
Taxis can be found easily in most major cities and resort towns. Meters are non-existent, so be sure to agree on your fare before you start your journey. Taxis can also be hired for cross-country trips.

Telephone
All telephone numbers in the Dominican Republic have seven digits. The national area code is 809. Public telephones are available, but usually require a phone card to access.

Time
The Dominican Republic maintains Eastern Standard Time (GMT minus five hours).

Tourist information
The main tourist body is the Dominican Republic Tourist Board.
   Residents of the UK should contact *The Dominican Republic Tourist Board, 18–22 Hands Court, High Holborn, London WC1X 7LF. Tel: (020) 7242 7778/0900 1600 305 for brochures. Email: inglaterra@sectur.gov.do*. In the US, contact *The Dominican Republic Tourist Board, 561 W Diversey Parkway, Suite 214, Chicago, IL 60614-1643. Tel: (773)*

A colourful *bureau de change*

529 1336. Email: chicago@sectur.gov.do. In Canada, contact *The Dominican Republic Tourist Board, 35 Church St, Unite 53, Market Square, Toronto, Ont. M5E 1T3. Tel: (416) 361 2126.*

Travellers with disabilities

Travellers with disabilities will find independent travelling extremely difficult. Some major monuments feature access ramps, but smaller hotels and public transport will offer absolutely no assistance mechanisms to help you get around. To enjoy your stay, stick with the larger, all-inclusive resorts.

Weather

Temperatures in the Dominican Republic do not vary much throughout the year. You can pretty much count on warm, sunny weather throughout your stay.

Hurricane season is a serious problem. From July through to mid-October, the island faces the possibility of extensive damage. Avoid travelling to the region in these months if possible.

Weather chart (averages) – Santo Domingo

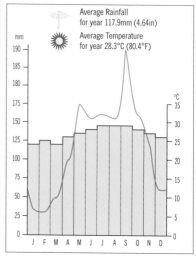

Weather chart (averages) – Puerto Plata

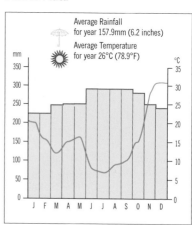

Sustainable Travel

Caring for Places we Visit

The Travel Foundation is a UK charity that cares for places we love to visit. You can help us protect the natural environment, traditions and culture – the things that make your visit special. And improve the well-being of local families – spreading the benefit of your visit to those who most need it. All of which can make your holiday experience even better! Most importantly, you can help ensure that there are great places for us all to visit – for generations to come.

What you can do:

• Remove any packaging from items before you go on holiday and recycle if possible.

• Do hire local guides and book locally-run excursions – it will enrich your holiday experience and help support local families.

• Hire a car only if you need to. Using public transport, bicycles and walking are environmentally-friendlier alternatives.

• Respect local culture and traditions. Ensure your dress and behaviour is appropriate for the places you visit. Ask permission before taking photographs of people or their homes.

• Turn down/off heating or air conditioning when not required. Switch off lights and turn the television off rather than leave on standby.

• Do use water sparingly. Take showers instead of baths and inform staff if you are happy to re-use towels and bed linen rather than replace daily.

• Don't pick flowers and plants or collect pebbles, seashells, coral or starfish. Leave them for others to enjoy.

• Don't buy products made from endangered plants or animals, including hardwoods, ivory, corals, reptiles or turtles. If in doubt – don't buy.

• Do buy locally-made products - shopping in locally-owned outlets and treating yourself to local food and drink is a great way to get into the holiday spirit and benefits local families.

• Always bargain with humour and bear in mind that a small cash saving to you could be a significant amount to the seller.

• Coral is extremely fragile. Don't step on or remove and avoid kicking up sand.

For more tips and information on The Travel Foundation and its work, please visit *www.thetravelfoundation.org.uk*.

the
travel foundation
caring for places we love to visit

ACKNOWLEDGEMENTS

Thomas Cook Publishing wishes to thank ETHEL DAVIES for the photographs reproduced in this book, to whom the copyright in the photographs belongs, with the exception of the following:

Bahia Principe San Juan hotelier, (page 174)
Dominican Republic Tourist Board (page 18, 112, 113 and 163)
HAPPY SURFPOOL CENTER, CABARETE, happycabarete.com, 001809 571 0784 (page 97a)
Iguana Mama (page 126 and 127)
Iguana Mama © Frédéric Mouchet (page 124)
Whale Samaná/Victoria Marine © Alejandro Avampini/www.aleava.net (page 88)
Whale Samaná/Victoria Marine © Silvan Wick (page 89)

Copy-editing: PENNY ISAACS

Index: INDEXING SPECIALISTS (UK) LTD

Maps: PC GRAPHICS, SURREY, UK

Proof-reading: CAMBRIDGE PUBLISHING MANAGEMENT LTD

Travellers

Feedback Form

Please help us improve future editions by taking part in our reader survey. Every returned form will be acknowledged. To show our appreciation we will send you a voucher entitling you to £1 off your next *Travellers* guide or any other Thomas Cook guidebook ordered direct from Thomas Cook Publishing. Just take a few minutes to complete and return this form to us.

We'd also be glad to hear of your comments, updates or recommendations on places we cover or you think that we ought to cover.

1. Which *Travellers* guide did you purchase?

_____

2. Have you purchased other *Travellers* guides in the series?

Yes ☐

No ☐

If Yes, please specify_____

3. Which of the following tempted you into buying your *Travellers* guide:
(Please tick as many as appropriate)

The price ☐

The cover ☐

The content ☐

Other_____

4. What do you think of :

a) the cover design? _____

b) the design and layout styles within the book?_____

c) the content _____

5. Please tell us about any features that in your opinion could be changed, improved or added in future editions of the book:

_____

_____

Your age category: ☐ under 21   ☐ 21-30   ☐ 31-40   ☐ 41-50   ☐ 51+

Mr/Mrs/Miss/Ms/Other

Surname_____ Initials_____

Full address: (Please include postal or zip code)_____

_____

Daytime telephone number: _____

Email address: _____

☐ Please tick here if you would be willing to participate in further customer surveys.

☐ Please tick here if you would like to receive information on new titles or special offers from Thomas Cook Publishing (please note we never give your details to third party companies).

Please detach this page and send it to: **The Editor, Travellers, Thomas Cook Publishing, PO Box 227, The Thomas Cook Business Park, Peterborough PE3 8SB, United Kingdom.**

tear along the perforation

The Editor, Travellers
Thomas Cook Publishing
PO Box 227
The Thomas Cook Business Park
Peterborough, PE3 8SB
United Kingdom